WHAT PEOPLE ARE SAYING ABOUT *GET IN THE GAME*

"Finally, it has arrived—the player's handbook for all walks of life for men. Jamie Holden has taken the sports analogy and written practical life applications with Bible support for every stage in a man's life. The added workbook is a bonus for men's small groups study. If you have ever played sports, you can relate to getting into a game. This book is a guideline for getting in the game of life."
—**Dr. Darrel Billups**, *National Coalition of Ministries to Men, Executive Director*

"Jamie has written a wonderful resource for any man who wants to be all God has created him to be. With sports metaphors and analogies, he has articulated so many of the essential elements needed by all of us men today who may be on the sidelines, be tempted to throw in the towel, or just be a spectator rather than being a part of the team that is committed to the work of the kingdom of God."
—**Dr. Stephen R. Tourville**, *PennDel Ministry Network Superintendent*

"Jamie Holden is an ace and definitely in his sweet spot when he writes, ***Get in the Game***! Jamie loves sports and uses it in an engaging way to help men get off the bench and become "Hall of Fame Heroes" in their family, church, community and workplace. One of the best parts of ***Get in the Game*** is that you can study it with your team of men—church softball team, guys you work with, your small accountability group—great stuff to help your team rise to championship caliber!"
—**Tom Rees**, *HonorBound Men's Director, PennDel Ministry Network*

JAMES J. HOLDEN

MORNING JOY MEDIA

Spring City, Pennsylvania

Published by Morning Joy Media. Visit www.morningjoymedia.com for more information on bulk discounts and special promotions, or e-mail your questions to info@morningjoymedia.com.

Design: Debbie Capeci
Author Photo (in back matter): Kristal Bentley

Subject Headings:
1. Christian life 2. Men's Issues 3. Spiritual formation.

ISBN 978-1-937107-61-1 (pbk)
ISBN 978-1-937107-62-8 (ebook)

Printed in the United States of America

This book is dedicated to a man who had the strength and courage to confront me at a dark time in my life when I was fumbling the ball, big time, spiritually. Jason Rising, your words to me at this time in my life were a launching point for me, starting my journey to becoming a godly man. Thank you for having the love and courage to help me see my weak areas so that I could begin to overcome and get in the game for God! You share in the legacy of anything God uses my life and ministry to do to reach other men struggling in their lives. I dedicate this book to you.

CONTENTS

PART 1 GETTING IN THE GAME

1 • CHOOSING TO GET OFF THE BENCH 1

PART 2 TRAINING CAMP

2 • LEARNING THE FUNDAMENTALS 11

3 • DRAFT DAY 25

4 • LEAVING THE OLD BEHIND.................................... 39

5 • PLAYING BY THE RULES 51

PART 3 MOMENTUM KILLERS

6 • NO PAIN, NO GAIN 71

7 • WINNERS NEVER CHEAT, AND CHEATERS NEVER WIN 85

8 • WINNING AGAINST COMPROMISE............................ 97

9 • SHINING A LIGHT ON THE DARK CORNERS.................... 111

10 • TRUTH IN BLACK & WHITE, AND ALL COLORS IN BETWEEN ... 129

11 • PLAYING THROUGH DISAPPOINTMENT.......................... 143

PART 4 BUILDING A DYNASTY

12 • THE VALUE OF A GOOD COACH 159

13 • BEING A TEAM PLAYER 173

14 • BUILDING THE TEAM FOR THE FUTURE................................ 183

SMALL GROUP WORKBOOK 195

CONTENTS

PART 1 GETTING IN THE GAME

PART 2 TRAINING

PART 4 BUILDING A DRAFT

SMALL GROUP WORKBOOK

PART 1 GETTING IN THE GAME

CHAPTER 1

CHOOSING TO
GET OFF THE BENCH

I have always loved sports. When I was a boy, the books I read were about sports stars. And now, I love watching sports on a day off. I enjoy fantasy baseball and football. Because of my disability, I have never been very good at playing sports. Actually, I was awful, but it didn't keep me from trying. I played Little League, where I was one of the best hitters on our team, but because of my disability, I couldn't run, and was often teased and ridiculed by the other team, my own teammates, and even parents in the stands. (This was in the days before participation trophies and rules restricting heckling from the grandstands.) Even my own coach was tough and borderline cruel because of my lack of abilities. Eventually, I quit the team.

However, my love of sports never died. I have been an avid fan of many sports over the years. As I said, I enjoy fantasy leagues. However, watching sports and being in fantasy leagues don't mean I am an athlete. I am fan of the game, but I am not in the game.

I enjoy watching the greatest athletes in the world compete against each other. I really enjoy watching epic battles like Tiger Woods vs.

Phil Mickelson, Tom Brady vs. Peyton Manning, a Yankees vs. Red Sox playoff series, or a LeBron James vs. Kevin Durant battle. It's epic watching Hall of Famers battle it out on the field of competition!

Just recently, the NFL held their Hall of Fame induction ceremony. I travel a lot, and to make the trips shorter I enjoy listening to sports talk radio. During the induction week, these shows had guest after guest talking about the thrill of making it to the Hall of Fame and sharing memories from their glory days. I was geeking out listening to their stories of success and victories.

The Hall of Fame is where you go to see the greatest of greats and to see their legacies. What don't you see there?

- Failures who get cut from teams
- Weaklings who couldn't make the team
- Guys who are banned from sports facilities
- Epic failures

Or do you?

Often we get so caught up in the glory and lore of these great athletes that we don't stop and look at where they came from or what they endured before they made it big. NBA superstar Michael Jordan, one of the greatest players in NBA history, did not make his varsity high school team the first year he tried out. New York Knicks superstar Carmelo Anthony was cut from his high school team. Bob Cousy, a six-time NBA champion, thirteen-time All-Star, Hall of Famer, and one of the fifty greatest players in NBA history, was cut his freshman year of high school!

One of the greatest PGA golfers ever, Tiger Woods, was forbidden to play many courses growing up because he was black.

NFL star wide receiver Wes Welker almost never got started with his five-time pro-bowl career because he was cut for being too short. Kurt Warner, NFL and Superbowl MVP, was unable to survive past training camp his rookie year. He was forced to find work elsewhere, with the well-known story of him stocking shelves at a local grocery store for near minimum wage.

MLB superstar ace pitcher Orel Hershiser was cut from both his high school and college baseball teams. He refused to let it get the best of him and built an eighteen-year career that included three All-Star appearances and one Cy Young Award.

Soccer superstar Lionel Messi was cut from junior league because he was said to be too short to be successful as a soccer player.

Most, if not all, of these men are destined to be in or are already in their respective sports Hall of Fame because they didn't let what others told them or what they felt about themselves keep them from getting in the game. They persevered, overcame, and the rest is history.

A few years back, I attended a conference where Mark Batterson was one of the speakers. During his message he said, "I am all for people going to church—I am a pastor, go to church. But if you think that is where the game is, you're wrong! That's the locker room. Monday through Friday you have to go out into the playing field and deliver!"

His words are so true! Too many people think they are in the game. But they aren't. They are sitting in the locker room.

For some, they are content to just sit in the locker room in their uniforms and feel like they are part of the team. Others are fans of the game, faithfully supporting the Christian leaders they draft in fantasy Christianity leagues, but they aren't in the game themselves.

Guys, we need to step out of the locker room and get in the game.

Many men aren't even suited up at all. They have let fear and the lies of the enemy keep them from becoming the victorious Christians God has created them to be.

Have you gotten into the game? I don't mean do you go to church regularly or do you follow a list of dos and don'ts for believers. I mean have you suited up and hopped into the action? Have you let your own opinion of your worth or the opinion of others sideline you?

Guys, we need to step out of the locker room and get in the game. We need to follow the playbook laid out for us in Matthew 28:19–20:

> *Therefore go and make disciples of all nations, baptizing them in the name of the Father and of the Son and of the Holy Spirit, and teaching them to obey everything I have commanded you.*

That's the X's and O's of Christianity. Get out there and make a difference. Win one for the Gipper (hmm…is it sacrilege to call God the Gipper?) We need to suit up, get out of the locker room, and change the world!

Too often we are the ones stopping ourselves from getting into the game. How many times have you thought to yourself, "Is there any way God can use a man like me?"

Honestly, we know ourselves better than anyone else. We know our struggles, our insecurities, our weaknesses, and our areas of sin, and often we feel useless to God because of them. We see who we really are, yet we long to be useful to God and to serve him and his kingdom. Frustrated, we look at the mess that is our lives and we scream, "God, can you do anything with me?!?"

God can use any man who is willing to be used! He wants you in the game, making a difference for his kingdom.

I am here to tell you, God can use any man who is willing to be used!

It doesn't matter who you are, where you came from, what you have done, or what you are struggling with, there is hope for you! God can take you and make you into a useful vessel in his kingdom!

I feel the message God has for his men is that he has a plan for your life! He wants you in the game, making a difference for his kingdom.

You know who else knows this? Our spiritual enemy!

The enemy is beating up God's men, making them feel too lost, too messed up, too far gone to be used by him. The enemy is keeping them trapped in the safety of the locker room.

The goal of this book is to be a source of encouragement to all my spiritual brothers to stop believing the enemy's lies. Guys, no matter where you came from, what you have done, or what you struggle with, God can use you! He can restore you. He can heal you. He can help you overcome and gain the victory. He can put you into the starting lineup and use you to change the world. How can I say this with such confidence?

I say it so boldly because the Bible is packed with the stories of average, ordinary men with real issues, real struggles, and real inadequacies that God took and transformed and used to change the world. Like a great cloud of witnesses, these men's lives are shining beacons of hope to us all that God can use us mightily for his kingdom. In this book, we will study the lives of some of these men.

We're also going to study some men in the Bible who did not reach their full potential in God's kingdom. Together, we'll look at the weaknesses that sidelined them from the game, made them fumble the ball, and kept them from becoming the world changers God intended them to be.

Why are we looking at both the winners and losers in the game of life?

So we can learn from their examples, learn from their mistakes, and make different choices in our own lives. Just as athletes watch game tapes to improve their performance and develop strategy, as Christians we need to watch the tapes of those who have gone before us so we can develop a strategy to avoid the pitfalls that destroyed lives, learn to overcome the enemy's destructive tactics, and create game plans to live a victorious life that leaves a legacy.

But we're not just going to focus on those who failed. Along the way, we'll also look at men who faced the same challenges but overcame. Men who were knocked down but got back up. Along the way, we will see that the greatness God did in and through them was done despite their weaknesses. Each of them had issues of their own that should have disqualified them for service, yet God looked past these issues to the heart of each man, and he saw something there he could work with. He challenged each man to let him do a changing work inside of them, and we will see what God did and how they became men God used mightily.

As we begin this journey together, we must commit to openly and honestly ask ourselves, "How am I like this man? Is there an area of my life that needs to be revolutionized in order to be used by God? Will I allow God to use me, or will I continue to take refuge and shelter in my own perceived inadequacies? Am I content sitting in the locker room, or do I want to feel the rush of stepping onto the field and getting into the game?"

At the end of each chapter there will be a Training Drill that's geared to helping you grow in the particular area we examined. It will also list another drill called Two-A-Days. Two-A-Days are when a team or individual trains on two separate occasions during the same day. Two-A-Days are used primarily to get in shape for the season. They are an extreme, intensive training. That's what these drills are for: more in-depth, deeper drills to help you grow in the area we discussed in the chapter.

Each chapter will end with the Team Meeting, which is a set of group study questions. I love the concept of men getting together and working through a book together, and these questions are geared to help start a discussion of the character traits in the chapter. I hope you use these questions in a group setting or at least work through them at home on your own.

These questions will also be listed in the back of the book in our workbook section so you don't have to constantly flip back and forth to the chapter when studying together. The workbook also has some questions designed for self-examination, and they include plenty of space for you to write your answers.

Finally, the workbook has Bulletin Board Material for each chapter. In sports, Bulletin Board Material is a comment or quote made in print that is used as a little bit of extra motivation. The coach uses a thumbtack and posts the snipped article up on the locker room bulletin board for everyone to read. The workbook will contain one key thought to meditate on and/or memorize.

Guys, I believe this book, filled with easy-to-read chapters, is going to be a life-changing book for the men who read it. God wants to use ordinary you to do extraordinary things for his kingdom. Are you ready to suit up and get in the game?

TRAINING DRILL

Will you commit to:

Reading each chapter, including Scripture verses? Yes/No

Praying the prayers at the end of the chapter? Yes/No

Completing the homework assignments? Yes/No

Sincerely examining your heart against the questions at the end of each chapter? Yes/No

TWO-A-DAYS

Commit to working through this book with a group of guys. Work together to get in the game!

TEAM MEETING

1. What does it mean to you to "get in the game"?

2. What is the difference between going to church and getting in the game?

3. What is the biggest obstacle to overcome in your life to get in the game?

4. Will we as a group commit to not only getting in the game but working together to win?

5. How can we as a group help you to get in the game?

PART 2
TRAINING CAMP

CHAPTER 2

LEARNING THE FUNDAMENTALS

"I think it's time I started an exercise routine."

That's what I said a few years ago when I approached my sister about my desire to purchase a Bowflex machine.

Her response, "Are you kidding? There's no way we can afford it!"

I replied, "But 'Dess, I really believe the Holy Spirit is challenging me to start an exercise program that would be good for my body but also relieve a lot of my mental stress. With my foot making it difficult for me to walk, I really believe this would be the best way for me to exercise."

So we started looking at the cost of exercise equipment online.

Quickly we realized that we were both right. The Bowflex machine was a good choice for me; however, we still didn't have the money.

So we shelved the idea—sort of. Over the course of the next week we talked about it, but we weren't sure how we could do more than that.

Then God did a miracle.

I remember we were out running errands—grocery shopping, returning items. I think Adessa was at Staples purchasing office supplies when I decided to go into a sporting goods store just to look around. While I was browsing, a gentleman came up to me and said, "I retired a few weeks ago and the people at my office gave me this gift card to buy golf equipment. Now that I'm here I see that this store doesn't sell the type of equipment I prefer, so if you want the gift card you can have it."

I was shocked, but I thanked the man and we both went on our way.

It wasn't until we called the toll-free number to see how much the gift card was worth that we realized what an incredible miracle had just occurred. Turns out, the gift card was worth almost $500! When we combined that gift card with a coupon that arrived in my email inbox that afternoon, we were able to purchase the Bowflex machine that I wanted and only pay for part of the shipping!

Talk about a miracle!

At a time in my life when I really needed an outlet to improve my physical and mental fitness, God literally *gave* me the equipment that would help me meet my goals. Years later, I still use the machine to help me strengthen my body and relax my mind. What an incredible blessing!

Still, there's one thing that I've learned about exercise equipment. While it was an amazing miracle and a reason for celebration that God provided our family with this machine, having the machine in our house didn't automatically make us physically fit. (I know, disappointing, isn't it?) The fact is that having this machine all set up in our basement, looking strong and shiny, doesn't do anything to improve anyone's body or relax anyone's mind. It's only when I take time out of my busy life, go downstairs, and use the machine the way it was intended that it does me any good.

The same thing that's true in the physical realm with the Bowflex machine that God gave our family is true in the spiritual realm.

In order for us to truly get in the game, we have to start with the fundamentals. Across our country, baseball, football, soccer fields, and basketball courts are full of coaches teaching kids the fundamentals of their sports. They teach them how to tackle, how to field a ground ball, how to do a corner kick, and how to dribble a basketball. These are fundamentals to the sport—if you don't learn them, you will never succeed in the game. The same is true for us. We need to learn the fundamentals of being a man of God. The two fundamentals we are going to look at in this chapter are prayer and Bible reading.

"Great, here we go, a guilt trip on not reading the Bible or praying enough!"

Wrong! I am not here to make anyone feel guilty. If you feel anything, it isn't from me. However, it could be conviction from the Holy Spirit. Why?

Well, here's the thing—even though God made these spiritual disciplines available to us, just like the Bowflex machine has no value unless it is used, the spiritual disciplines God has given do not benefit our spiritual lives unless we discipline ourselves to consistently use them.

That's why I believe the Holy Spirit led me to add this chapter. It really is key to getting in the game. Any athlete will tell you that if you don't excel in the fundamentals, you won't last long in the game.

As I said, this will not be a series of guilt trips condemning you for not spending enough time in prayer or reading the Bible. (Because let's be honest, guilt trips have never motivated anyone.)

Instead, this chapter will help you explore and understand the benefits of prayer and Bible reading and will whet your appetite to give these spiritual disciplines a try and see how they benefit your spiritual life. Because ultimately, that's what it's about—the healthy growth that each of us can gain from spiritual exercise, not just going through the motions out of guilt.

1 Timothy 4:8 says, *"For physical training is of some value, but godliness has value for all things, holding promise for both the present life and the life to come."*

I like the way *The Message* puts it, *"Exercise daily in God—no spiritual flabbiness, please! Workouts in the gymnasium are useful, but a disciplined life in God is far more so, making you fit both today and forever."*

We need to get in shape and learn how to excel at these two fundamentals. Let's get started.

GET ON YOUR KNEES AND FIGHT LIKE A MAN

Prayer is the third greatest gift that God has ever given to us. Salvation is first, followed by the Holy Spirit. Then, in my opinion, comes prayer. Why?

There is power when God's men pray! It's rightly been said that the number one sign of a godly man is calloused knees.

There is power when God's men pray. Our prayers could change the world if only we took time to pray them.

James 5:16 says, *"The prayer of a righteous person is powerful and effective."*

Our prayers could change the world if only we took time to pray them. Satan knows it. This is why he will attempt anything to keep us from connecting with God in prayer. He knows how powerful it is, because he knows how powerful God is and that God will back us up when we ask him for help. Prayer is how we keep our spiritual lives thriving. We have to keep our spiritual fire burning. The main fuel for this fire is prayer.

Prayer is a lot like a gas grill we use to cook our food when we barbecue.

God is the propane tank that supplies the fuel, the passion, the fire.

We are the grill that cooks the food, which does the work of ministry, witnessing, serving, and living for God.

Prayer is the gas line that connects the tank to the grill.

Without the gas line, the tank has no way to fuel the grill. The gas line connects the two parts together and produces a flame. When we pray, our prayers connect us to the heart of God. God gives us what we need to serve him and reach others with the gospel. We can only excel in the game when we learn how to pray.

Along with prayer, God's men should learn to read and apply the Word of God. Why? Let me illustrate it to you using a story from my life.

When I was younger, my family attended an event at the Nassau Coliseum in Long Island, New York. The event ended around 11 p.m., and the plan was to drive to a hotel in New Jersey to get some sleep before we toured New York City the next day. However, our plans changed when my dad missed the exit he was supposed to take and our tour started earlier than we'd planned (and without a tour guide).

The only thing was that our unplanned tour didn't lead us toward the common tourist attractions. Instead, our naïve little family from the country spent the next four hours driving through the various boroughs of New York seeing places and things we'd never seen before. (Imagine the Beverly Hillbillies meet Queens, New York—now you've got a good picture.)

We were lost! Remember this was before GPS and cell phones were owned by the average person. There was a brief ray of light when we saw a group of police cars parked together and we thought we could stop and ask for directions. We were wrong! Apparently, policemen in certain boroughs of New York get very nervous when cars pull up directly beside them in the wee hours of the morning. They were not happy! As the clock crept past midnight and into 1 a.m., then 2 a.m., I think my parents would have given anything for a map, a GPS, or even a friendly police officer who would give us directions to get back on the right road. Since we didn't have any of these things, we just kept driving around and around, trying to find our way back to the hotel. (We did finally arrive around 3 a.m.—although I still don't remember how!)

What did I learn from this event? Directions are important! Keep a map in your car so you don't end up in dangerous situations for which you are totally unprepared.

Come to think of it—that's not a bad motto for life. The only thing is that life, no matter how dangerous it can be or how unprepared we are to face its challenges, doesn't come with a roadmap.

Or does it?

Thankfully, the answer is, "Yes, it does."

That's why it's so important that we read the Bible every day. Essentially, it's our owner's manual for how to successfully navigate the roads of life. Putting it into sports terms, it is the game film we watch to learn how to defeat the opponent.

The Bible is full of men who have gone before us, and we can learn valuable keys to avoiding the sins and traps that try to defeat us from their stories. As we continue through the rest of the chapters in this book, we will look at individual men and learn from their game film. But first we have to learn the fundamentals. We need to become men who love the Bible. Why?

It's simple. The Bible is the Word of God.

As the Creator of the universe, God understands how the universe works.

Graciously, he has shared these keys to successful living with us in his Word.

When we read his Word and apply these keys to our lives, we will prosper and succeed spiritually, emotionally, mentally, and even in our practical lives. Essentially, the Bible tells us how to live life the way God intended it to be lived. It truly is a fundamental we need to learn.

But let's be real and honest with each other. More than likely, you already know reading the Bible on a daily basis is important. Most of us do not struggle with the question of "Why should I read the Bible?" Instead, we struggle more with the actual doing of what we know is right.

I have to admit, this is an area where I've struggled throughout my life. Since I was a child, there have been times when I've been red-hot and passionately committed to reading the Bible. There've also been other seasons where I simply didn't make Bible reading a priority. Although I knew it was important, I put it at the end of the list of "things to do." As we all know, the things that fall into the "I'll get to them when I have time" category rarely get done.

So I get how easy it is to fall into the excuse of "too busy to read the Bible." However, just because I understand it doesn't make it right. Because whether it's you or me or the 90 percent of Protestants who wish they read the Bible more, the reality is that when we say "I don't have time to read the Bible," what we're really saying is that reading the Bible and learning God's ways aren't as important to you as the other things in your life. It isn't a priority, because we always make time for our priorities.

That's basically where the rubber meets the road when it comes to the truth about the spiritual discipline of daily Bible reading: **If we don't make it a top priority, it won't happen.**

Also, if we don't read the Bible, we're forfeiting all the benefits we can get from reading God's Word. Ultimately, because we won't know God's will and God's ways, we won't walk in them, and we'll make choices that will result in bad consequences in every area of our lives. That's why the best choice any man can make is the choice to read the Bible daily so he can learn God's principles as they are laid out in the Bible and apply them to his life.

Here are some practical tips I've learned to help us make this choice:

1. ACCOUNTABILITY.

The biggest thing that has ever helped me stick to my daily Bible reading during a time in life when it was a struggle was a friend or family member asking, "Did you read the Bible today?" That's why I suggest finding an accountability partner and checking in with each other daily or weekly. Encourage each other to make Bible reading a priority. Maybe you could even read through the same book of the Bible together and discuss it. Accountability is a powerful tool—use it!

Ecclesiastes 4:9–10 says, *"Two are better than one, because they have a good return for their labor: If either of them falls down, one can help the other up."*

2. CHOOSE A TRANSLATION YOU CAN UNDERSTAND.

The King James Version is not for everyone—neither is the New International Version. Choose a version that is readable for you and this will make the Bible reading process more productive and enjoyable.

3. CHOOSE TO READ THE BIBLE IN A DIFFERENT TRANSLATION ONCE IN A WHILE.

This tip is for those of you that have read the Bible so many times it's beginning to feel a little monotonous. A great way to shake things up is to try a different translation for a while. Personally, this year I am doing my Bible reading from *The Message* version. Reading in a different translation than I would usually use has been very beneficial to me. You'll be surprised how adding just a slightly different flavor may re-spark your enthusiasm.

4. CHOOSE TO READ SMALLER PORTIONS FROM DIFFERENT SECTIONS OF THE BIBLE.

I learned this from my mom, who would read a portion from the Old Testament, a portion from the New Testament, and a portion in Psalms every day. She encouraged me that following her pattern would help me stop avoiding Bible reading when I arrived at the genealogies or Leviticus.

She was right: her way really did help! Why? Because even though I might be reading through one part of the Bible that was a little tedious, I'd also be reading another part that wasn't. Variety is the spice of life!

5. COMMIT TO A DAILY BIBLE READING PLAN.

My sister Adessa shared this tip with me. She signed up for a daily Bible reading plan with biblegateway.com. Every day, they send the passages she is supposed to read to her email box. She is on track to read through the Bible again this year. I chose a plan from the Bible App, which has a daily reading from the Old Testament, New Testament, Psalms, and Proverbs. Other Bible reading plans are available online, in books, or through your local church. The important thing isn't which plan you choose, but that you choose a plan and stick with it.

6. DOWNLOAD THE BIBLE APP.

Here's an interesting statistic: Of adults who increased their Bible readership last year, one-quarter (26 percent) say it was due to having downloaded the Bible onto their smartphone or tablet.

Let me just add a whole-hearted "Amen!"

Because while I was at first skeptical of reading the Bible on your phone, I've recently come to realize that this is an amazingly valuable tool against the excuse of "I'm too busy to read the Bible."

Why?

Well, because we all have downtime. We've all got those blocks of time when we're waiting in an office, waiting in line, or waiting for someone to arrive.

What if, rather than using these blocks of time to check out Facebook or play Candy Crush, we'd use this time to read the Bible? Can you imagine the impact it would have on our day, our lives, and even the world around us?

This is a great way to prove that Bible reading is a priority in our lives without sacrificing any of the things that we really must do. In today's busy society, this is one of the best apps you can choose because it will produce the greatest rewards in your life.

7. LISTEN TO AN AUDIO BIBLE.

This is something I recently started doing. Okay, full disclosure: I started listening to an audio Bible because I found it funny how dramatically the guy read the text. That, with his semi-British accent (why do all Bible movies and CDs think the people in the Bible were British?) was really amusing to me. Not the best motivation to use this method, I know.

However, as I started listening, I found it was a really interesting method to do now and then. Hearing the text spoken is really different than reading it. It was a nice change of pace. Plus, I could play it on my phone and set a sleep timer and fall asleep to God's Word at night instead of the TV or music. An audio Bible shouldn't fully replace reading the Bible, but it is a nice switch to mix it up a bit!

8. JUST DO IT!

When it comes to the topic of daily Bible reading, there eventually comes a point where we need to stop making excuses, take a cue from Nike, and "Just Do It."

Start somewhere.

Commit to a Bible reading plan.

Determine that reading God's Word is important in your life, put it at the top of your priority list, and make time to do it.

It's when you make that decision that you'll start reaping the benefits of God's Word, building spiritual muscle, and finding strength for the journey.

Now that we have identified the need to get into the game and have looked at the fundamentals we need to excel at, we are going to start looking at different men in the Bible who teach us valuable lessons to help us not only get in the game, but stay in the game and win. Are you ready?

Dear heavenly Father, I am a man who is committed to getting off the bench and getting into the game. As I work toward a life of serving you, becoming the godly man you called me to be, and reaching those around me with the gospel, help me to develop and excel in the fundamentals.

Let this prayer be the first in the process of developing a prayer life as I connect my heart to yours through prayer. Help me as I commit myself to spending time in the Word. Bring your Word to life as I read it. Use it to convict, encourage, and strengthen me as I serve you. In Jesus' name, amen!

TRAINING DRILL

1. Download the Bible App to your smartphone or device.
2. Find a daily Bible reading plan from someplace like the Bible App or biblegateway.com and commit to reading the Bible daily.

TWO-A-DAYS

Read through the entire Psalm 119 and make a list of all the ways that the psalmist says God's Word makes a difference in our lives.

TEAM MEETING

1. Why are the fundamentals so important?

2. How is your prayer life?

3. How can we as a group help you grow your prayer life?

4. Which of the eight points listed on how to read the Bible do you already use?

5. Which of the eight points are you going to start using?

6. How can we as a group help you develop the fundamentals?

CHAPTER 3

DRAFT DAY

After the Super Bowl has ended, the confetti has been thrown, the interviews have concluded, and the celebrating is over, the thoughts of NFL fans across the globe begin to drift toward the future and wonder, "What will happen in the next season of the NFL?"

We wonder what teams will change, what teams will remain the same. Will my favorite player retire (Peyton! Sniff, sniff) or be traded? Where will the free agents go? One of the highlights in this game of predictions and forecasts comes in April as all tune in to watch the NFL draft.

For those of you who are less football-minded, the NFL draft is an elaborate event where teams choose which of the top college players will go to their team. Draft night always has drama as players fall down the board or some team jumps up to get a specific player. Few forget the drama over whether Peyton Manning or Ryan Leaf would be the first overall pick so many years ago. (Can you believe that was even a topic??) Then there was the night everyone waited to see if Eli Manning, Peyton's brother, would actually play for the team that drafted him or insist on a trade. Giants fans were thankful he chose the latter. Who can forget the famous draft of Tim Tebow in the first round when many predicted no one would pick him? These were nights to remember!

I'll never forget when my Denver Broncos drafted Von Miller a few years ago. This turned out to be an awesome pick as he went on to be the MVP in Super Bowl 50 this past season.

But let's take a moment and play "let's pretend."

Let's say that, on the night of the draft, Von Miller got the call to play for the Denver Broncos but he refused to answer the phone. Let's imagine that his name and number were called, but instead of going to the stage, jumping at the chance of a lifetime to see his dream come true, he had his manager stand up and say, "Sorry, we've thought about it, but no thanks."

What if he did some soul searching, weighed his options and decided the rewards of playing in the NFL weren't worth the sacrifices he'd have to make?

Even though he'd still be famous (because the media would go crazy over the stupidity of his decision), he wouldn't have seen his dream come true. He wouldn't have played in a Super Bowl, he never would have been named MVP, and he'd have lost all the rewards of being a professional football player. Instead, he'd be known as the man who could have had it all, but said, "No thanks—not my thing."

We'd have all said, "All that talent and opportunity! What a waste!"

Now obviously, this didn't happen.

However, something very similar does happen over and over again as God's men are offered the opportunity to play on God's team and fulfill their destiny and they say, "No thanks—it's just too much sacrifice."

Without even very much thought, they give away the opportunity of lifetime. They could have it all, but instead, they choose to walk away rather than commit to going all in with God.

One Christmas about ten years ago, I received a book from my mom and dad. It was by one of my heroes of the faith, Fred Stoeker. The book was called *Every Man's Challenge*. The subtitle of the book posed an interesting question. "How far are you willing to go for God?"

That is a great question. It is a question that all men need to face. In this chapter, we are going to try and fully understand this question and see all of its implications. We will do this by examining the story of a man who could have been Jesus' thirteenth disciple. However, his inability to go all the way for God kept him from having a deep relationship with God. He could have had the great opportunity of serving and learning side by side with Jesus, but because of his divided heart, he ended up sad, alone, and apart from God. His story is a clear warning against allowing things to stand between us and God. Let's get started.

THE MAN JESUS WOULD HAVE MADE A DISCIPLE

Most people who are familiar with the four Gospels know that John was often known as "the disciple whom Jesus loved." However, in the Gospel of Luke we see that this title was almost stolen by another man who came seeking out Jesus. To see his story, let's look at Luke 18:18.

> *A certain ruler asked him, "Good teacher, what must I do to inherit eternal life?"*

We read this man was a ruler. In other Gospel accounts, we read that he was a younger man. Being a ruler meant he was a leader of the local synagogue. He would have been a well-respected, influential, righteous man who was known by many people. This is what makes it so odd that he came to Jesus asking this question.

First of all, the rulers weren't really Jesus' biggest fans. Most of them hated his guts!

Second, to the average onlooker, it seemed he was the model of the man who deserved eternal life. If there was a Who's Who of Eternal

Life, most would assume this guy's name would be toward the top of the list.

Many observing this scene probably wondered if he was just another leader trying to make a name for himself by questioning Jesus. He certainly wasn't the first person to throw a theology question at Jesus, trying to expose him as less than holy. However, as we read on, we see that Jesus didn't look suspiciously at the man. He didn't throw a "woe" at him as he often did to rulers and Pharisees. Instead, he looked him in the eye and sincerely answered the question.

> *"Why do you call me good?" Jesus answered. "No one is good—except God alone. You know the commandments: 'You shall not commit adultery, you shall not murder, you shall not steal, you shall not give false testimony, honor your father and mother.'"*

Jesus, knowing this young man thought a lot of himself, tried to direct his attention to the fact that no human could be labeled "good." All men are sinners. Only God is truly good. If Jesus wouldn't take this praise for himself as God's Son, then this man definitely had no right to think this way about himself.

Jesus instead reminds the man that the only way to be labeled "good" is to totally and completely obey the Law of Moses. Since this is impossible, the only conclusion to be reached is that no one can do anything to obtain salvation. It can only come through the one good person, God. As we read on, we see that the young ruler totally misses Jesus' point.

> *"All these I have kept since I was a boy," he said.*

Wow! How's that for an arrogant statement! In essence, he is saying he has never done anything wrong. He felt he lived a truly holy life. Spiritually, he thought he was the man! He did the deeds, said the prayers, made the required sacrifices. He had arrived spiritually, on to eternal life!

This young man had a wrong view of salvation and righteousness. He felt it came from obeying a list of rules and regulations. He failed to recognize that salvation and eternal life only come through admitting our needs, turning to God for forgiveness of our sins, and devoting our lives to being God's servants. He had a lot to learn, and Jesus was about to take him to school.

Let's switch to Mark's Gospel now. Remember, Mark was mentored by Peter; he wrote his Gospel based on Peter's first-hand observations. In Mark's account we see something that only someone there could notice. Let's look at Mark 10:21.

Jesus looked at him and loved him.

What an awesome statement. Jesus loved this young man. He saw great potential for this young ruler's life and ministry. He saw inside of this man a serious desire to learn the truth. Jesus wanted this young man to be one of his disciples. However, he had to see if the young man was serious about following him or not. He poses an interesting situation to the young man.

He is issuing a challenge for this young man to lay aside everything else in his life and serve Jesus wholeheartedly. Unfortunately, the young man's heart was divided.

Jesus looked at him and loved him. "One thing you lack," he said. "Go, sell everything you have and give to the poor, and you will have treasure in heaven. Then come, follow me."

Basically, Jesus is calling this young man's name in the draft. He is issuing a challenge for this young man to lay aside everything else in his life and serve Jesus wholeheartedly. Unfortunately, the young man's heart was divided.

At this the man's face fell. He went away sad, because he had great wealth.

On the one hand, he wanted to serve God and live the life of a disciple, yet he also wanted to hang on to his normal, familiar way of life. For this man, his normal life was a rich, luxurious lifestyle. However, the money isn't the issue here. Money is never the issue. The real issue is the heart of the man.

He wanted to serve God the way he wanted to do it. He wanted to stay comfortable. He didn't want to change his ways.

Most of all, he didn't want to surrender everything to God. He would go part way, but he held back. Full, unconditional surrender was not an option.

Jesus asked him to go too far, further than he was willing. As a result, he left sad, hopeless, and alone. He had a chance to have the ultimate experience, serving side by side with Jesus, to be remembered throughout all of history as the thirteenth disciple, but his heart was divided. Guys, we must make sure we don't make the same mistake.

You may be thinking, "Jamie, you have nothing to worry about. I don't have a lot of money, so it won't come between me and God."

Money is not the issue we are discussing. Most of us have never been in a position of great wealth. However, we all have things in our lives that, left unchecked, can keep our hearts divided from fully following God. What if God approached you and asked these things of you?

What if God asked you to give up your fifteen minutes in the morning reading Facebook and replace it with Bible reading?

Would you be willing to give up your favorite TV show if God began to show you that he didn't approve of it?

If God asked you not to play fantasy football for a season and instead volunteer to lead a group of teens at your church, would you give it up?

If you were offered the job of your dreams that you had been working so hard to achieve, would you turn it down because God wants you spending more time with both him and your family?

How about this (this actually happened to a preacher I knew): You are saving up to buy a new car. You have an older car that is still in good shape, but you are going to buy a new one. You decide to sell your old one and use the money toward a new car. You figure you can get about $3,000 for your old one, which is a nice down payment for the new one. However, you feel God tell you to give the old car to a poor man who needs a car to drive to work and support his family. Would you lay down that much for God?

Deciding to answer God's draft call is an issue we all must face. In order to reach our full potential as God's men, we must be willing to hold nothing back.

This is a decision I have had to face in my life. Multiple times God has asked me how far I am willing to go for him. One time God asked me to give up the only sport I was ever good at, golf. Because of my physical problems, I was not a good athlete. This caused tremendous damage to my self-image. I grew up in an area where to be a "real man" you had to be athletic. Golf was the only sports outlet that filled this image. God asked me to totally give up golf and get my

> **While it hurts to cut out the things that cause a divided heart, it in no way equals the pain and disappointment that we endure when we realize that we could have had more with God.**

sense of self-worth through him. It was hard, but looking back now, it was well worth it.

This is just a small example of the many ways God tests us to see if we have a divided heart. I have had to give up dreams, aspirations, relationships, thought patterns, and even the image I tried to present to people in order to wholeheartedly follow God. He hasn't let me keep anything that keeps me from wholeheartedly following him. For this I am thankful. While it hurts to cut out the things that cause a divided heart, it in no way equals the pain and disappointment that we endure when we realize that we could have had more with God.

The rich young ruler shows us the grief of allowing our hearts to stay divided. We must choose to surrender everything to God.

Need someone to look to for inspiration?

A great example of a man who, unlike this young ruler, did give it all up to follow Jesus was Peter. Peter left his life as a fisherman, his security, everything he had, to follow Jesus.

After the rich young ruler walked away from Jesus, Jesus began to teach about how hard it is for anyone to follow him. Few will pay the price as demonstrated by this young ruler. However, not all refuse to pay it. Many are willing to follow Jesus wholeheartedly. Peter was one of them. Let's look at Mark 10 again, verse 28–30:

> *Then Peter spoke up, "We have left everything to follow you!"*
> *"Truly I tell you," Jesus replied, "no one who has left home or brothers or sisters or mother or father or children or fields for me and the gospel will fail to receive a hundred times as much in this present age: homes, brothers, sisters, mothers, children and fields— along with persecutions—and in the age to come eternal life.*

Here were two men, one was a fan of Jesus, and the other was totally committed, sold out, and following him wholeheartedly. Jesus' final words above ring true today. The rich young ruler and his divided heart died, and along with him all of his wealth. Peter, on the other hand, went 100 percent in with Jesus, leaving everything behind.

Two thousand years later, Peter is a Christian rock star! He wrote two books of the Bible and also is responsible for telling Mark the contents of the Gospel of Mark. Many lives have been changed through Peter's life. The same can't be said of the ruler with a divided heart.

As we bring this chapter to a close, I want to share one last story with you.

There was once a cheerful little boy named Johnny who was almost five. Waiting with his mother at the checkout stand, he saw it: a shiny, plastic, miniature football. "Oh please, Mommy. Can I have it? Please, Mommy, please!" Quickly the mother checked the tag on the little football and then looked back into the pleading eyes of her little guy's upturned face. "A dollar ninety-five. That's almost two dollars. If you really want it, I'll think of some extra chores for you and in no time you can save enough money to buy it for yourself. Your birthday's only a week away and you might get another crisp dollar bill from Grandma."

As soon as Johnny got home, he emptied his penny bank and counted out seventeen pennies. After dinner, he did more than his share of chores and he went to the neighbor and asked her if he could pick dandelions for ten cents. On his birthday, his Grandma did give him another new dollar bill and at last he had enough money to buy the football.

Johnny loved his football. It made him feel cool and grown up. He took it everywhere—Sunday school, kindergarten, even to bed. It never left his side.

Johnny had a very loving dad and every night when he was ready for bed, he would stop whatever he was doing and come upstairs to read him a story. One night when he finished the story, he asked Johnny, "Do you love me?"

"Oh yes, Daddy. You know that I love you."

"Then give me your football."

"Oh, Daddy, not my football. But you can have my soldier—the one dressed in camo from my collection. The one with the machine gun. Remember, Daddy? The one you gave me. He's my favorite."

"That's okay, buddy. Daddy loves you. Good night." And he brushed his cheek with a kiss.

About a week later, after the story time, Johnny's daddy asked again, "Do you love me?"

"Daddy, you know I love you."

"Then give me your football."

"Oh Daddy, not my football. But you can have my dump truck. The brand new one I got for my birthday. You can even have the rocks that came with it."

"That's okay. Sleep well. God bless you, little one. Daddy loves you."

A few nights later when his dad came in, Johnny was sitting cross-legged on his bed. As he came close, he noticed his chin was trembling and one silent tear rolled down his cheek.

"What is it, Johnny? What's the matter?"

Johnny didn't say anything but lifted his little hand up to his daddy. In his hand was the plastic football. With a little quiver, he finally said, "Here, Daddy. It's for you."

With tears gathering in his own eyes, Johnny's kind dad reached out with one hand to take the dime-store football, and with the other hand he reached under the bed and pulled out a genuine leather, official NFL football and gave it to Johnny. He had it all the time. He was just waiting for Johnny to give up the dime-store stuff so he could give him genuine treasure. So much like our heavenly Father. What are you hanging on to?

What is keeping you from answering God's draft call and the blessing of becoming God's man?

Is there sin that you are holding on to?

Is there something that you are holding on to, something that you won't surrender to God?

Will you surrender it to God?

Will you give up that plastic football so God can give you his real football?

What are you willing to give up for God?

What are you willing to separate yourself from for him?

Maybe you have never accepted Christ into your heart. He is waiting now for you to come to him. Or maybe you are a Christian who just hasn't been surrendered to God. You want all of God that you can have, but you are holding on to that one sin, that one action, that one relationship.

Please, right now, surrender your life to God. Surrender your will. Follow God wholeheartedly. Only then can you have God's presence in a way that you never thought possible. Only then can you experience victory.

The rich young ruler held on to his money and never entered into a full relationship with God. His divided heart kept him from going all the way. You can make a different choice. You can choose today to answer God's call and get in the game.

Dear heavenly Father, please forgive me for allowing myself to have a divided heart. Please show me what things are keeping me from going as far as I can with you. Give me the strength to surrender these things to you. Help me learn from the example of the rich young ruler. Develop in me a heart that follows after you wholeheartedly. I want to go all the way for you. In Jesus' name, amen.

TRAINING DRILL

Ask God to reveal to you areas where you are not wholeheartedly following him.

Make a list of any areas that are not completely surrendered to God. Then repent of them and make any necessary changes.

TWO-A-DAYS

Ask your mentor and/or a trusted friend or family member if he sees an area in your life where you are not wholeheartedly devoted to God or have a tendency to go back to your old life. Don't be defensive when he honestly answers you.

TEAM MEETING

1. What does it mean to follow God wholeheartedly?

2. What are some things that are dividing your heart?

3. We said the young ruler felt Christianity was following a list of rules and regulations. What is it really?

4. What is keeping you from the blessing of becoming God's man? Is there sin that you are holding on to? Is there something that you are holding on to, something that you won't surrender to God?

5. What are you willing to give up for God? What are you willing to separate yourself from for him?

6. How far will you go for God? Really, how far?

7. What stands out to you the most about the rich young ruler's story? What did you learn from studying his game footage to help you avoid the trap he fell into in his life?

8. How can we as a group help you?

CHAPTER 4

LEAVING THE OLD BEHIND

I love to read autobiographies and interviews of successful people. We can learn so many valuable lessons from others around us. Recently I was listening to an interview about an NFL superstar. This athlete was retiring from the NFL, and many sports shows and radio talk shows were talking about this man and his legacy.

The player was a defensive powerhouse. He was feared, but more importantly, he was respected. He was a team leader, a mentor to the younger players, and the ultimate motivator. People talked about this amazing man's influence both on and off the field. They were all amazed at the man he had become. Why?

Because when he first entered the league, he was a mess. He was always in trouble, culminating in a bar fight with life-changing effects to those involved. It was at this point that the player had to make a choice. He could leave his old life and friends behind him and dedicate himself to excelling at the game he loved, or he could hold on to his past and his old relationships, and continue to be dragged down, and eventually be out of the game.

He chose to leave it behind and surround himself with good relationships as he strove to become the best athlete he could be. His choice was the difference between being a college bust or a future Hall of Famer. He had to let go of his past to excel in his future.

Guys, the same the same is true for us. What do I mean? To explain, we are going to look at the story of a man in the Bible who was told by God to leave everything behind him, but who instead allowed one little thing to come with him. Who is this man? His name is Abraham.

We have to let go of our past to excel in our future.

Wait! Abraham? The patriarch of the Jewish nation? The man God made a covenant with to become God's chosen people? The man whose lineage brought us the Messiah? The Hebrews 11 hero-of-the-faith Abraham? That guy?

Yup! That is the guy we are going to look at today. While Abraham was greatly blessed by God, he did make mistakes along the way that we can all look at and learn from. That is what we are going to do today. Let's dive in!

Genesis 12:1–3 tells us, "*The LORD had said to Abram, 'Go from your country, your people and your father's household to the land I will show you. "I will make you into a great nation, and I will bless you; I will make your name great, and you will be a blessing. I will bless those who bless you, and whoever curses you I will curse; and all peoples on earth will be blessed through you."'*"

In this passage we read God's original call and plan for Abram, whom he renamed Abraham, and his life. God tells him where to go, what to do, and how he would bless him. Let's see Abraham's response to God's command.

So Abram went, as the LORD had told him; and Lot went with him.

Notice the words in this passage. Abraham obeyed and did what God told him to do. However, he took someone along with him from his past. Even though God told him to leave his father and his family, Abraham took his nephew Lot with him.

God never called Lot to go along with Abraham. He wanted Abraham to leave everything behind and follow him wholeheartedly. Abraham did this, but he let Lot come along on this new spiritual journey with God.

Lot was never part of God's plan, and his accompanying Abraham caused Abraham nothing but grief. Let's look at Genesis 13:1–7 to see what I mean.

So Abram went up from Egypt to the Negev, with his wife and everything he had, and Lot went with him. Abram had become very wealthy in livestock and in silver and gold.

From the Negev he went from place to place until he came to Bethel, to the place between Bethel and Ai where his tent had been earlier and where he had first built an altar. There Abram called on the name of the LORD.

Now Lot, who was moving about with Abram, also had flocks and herds and tents. But the land could not support them while they stayed together, for their possessions were so great that they were not able to stay together. And quarreling arose between Abram's herders and Lot's. The Canaanites and Perizzites were also living in the land at that time.

In these verses we see Abraham begin to realize the blessings and promises God had on his life. He is growing and becoming wealthy and prosperous. However, his choice to bring Lot along from his old life began to interfere with the blessings God was pouring out on his life. Lot's people were fighting Abraham's household and causing strife, divisions, and issues for Abraham. Eventually, he had to deal with the situation.

> *So Abram said to Lot, "Let's not have any quarreling between you and me, or between your herders and mine, for we are close relatives. Is not the whole land before you? Let's part company. If you go to the left, I'll go to the right; if you go to the right, I'll go to the left."*
>
> *Lot looked around and saw that the whole plain of the Jordan toward Zoar was well watered, like the garden of the LORD, like the land of Egypt. (This was before the LORD destroyed Sodom and Gomorrah.) So Lot chose for himself the whole plain of the Jordan and set out toward the east. The two men parted company: Abram lived in the land of Canaan, while Lot lived among the cities of the plain and pitched his tents near Sodom.*

Because Abraham brought Lot with him, Lot got the pick of the land and Abraham didn't get the good land. However, God was still with Abraham, and, in the remainder of Genesis 13, God tells Abraham that he was going to bless him and give him the whole land. So even though Lot came with Abraham, the situation was resolved, and Lot had been only a minor annoyance for Abraham, right?

Wrong!

Shortly after the separation of Abraham and Lot, Abraham received disturbing news. Four kings had united and attacked the cities of Sodom and Gomorrah. Casualties were huge, and they gained victory. Not only that, but Lot had been taken captive.

Genesis 14, beginning in verse 11, says,

> *The four kings seized all the goods of Sodom and Gomorrah and all their food; then they went away. They also carried off Abram's nephew Lot and his possessions, since he was living in Sodom.*

A man who had escaped came and reported this to Abram the Hebrew. Now Abram was living near the great trees of Mamre the Amorite, a brother of Eshkol and Aner, all of whom were allied with Abram. When Abram heard that his relative had been taken captive, he called out the 318 trained men born in his household and went in pursuit as far as Dan. During the night Abram divided his men to attack them and he routed them, pursuing them as far as Hobah, north of Damascus. He recovered all the goods and brought back his relative Lot and his possessions, together with the women and the other people.

Abraham was forced to go and rescue Lot from the four kings that had taken him prisoner. You may be thinking, "So what, Abraham fought and won a great battle. He was the winner!"

While this is true, the point is this: Abraham was forced to engage in a battle and fight a war that he never would have had to fight if Lot hadn't come with him! The fact that he won isn't important. He never should have had to get involved at all!

The four kings attacking and conquering were probably used by God to weaken a strong city, so when the time came for Abraham to receive these cities as his possession, they would be weakened and easier for him to win. But because Lot came with him, he had to get involved in a battle that was none of his business or concern. So, once again, bringing Lot with him caused Abraham nothing but grief.

As you continue through the next four chapters of Genesis, it seems as if Lot is no longer a source of grief to Abraham. We read of God giving Abraham a promise of an heir and son. We read of God continuing to grow and prosper Abraham. It was a good period of time for Abraham. Then once again, Abraham's decision to let Lot come with him ends up biting him in the butt.

One day, twenty-four years after the decision to let Lot come with him, Abraham is visited by three men. One of the men is Jesus incarnate, and the other two are angels!

What a privilege for Abraham to have God in flesh appear to him! Jesus tells Abraham and Sarah they will have a son! It was a great, life-changing day. As Jesus and his angels got up to leave, they walked toward Sodom.

> *When the men got up to leave, they looked down toward Sodom, and Abraham walked along with them to see them on their way. Then the LORD said, "Shall I hide from Abraham what I am about to do? Abraham will surely become a great and powerful nation, and all nations on earth will be blessed through him. For I have chosen him, so that he will direct his children and his household after him to keep the way of the LORD by doing what is right and just, so that the LORD will bring about for Abraham what he has promised him."*
>
> *Then the LORD said, "The outcry against Sodom and Gomorrah is so great and their sin so grievous that I will go down and see if what they have done is as bad as the outcry that has reached me. If not, I will know."*
>
> *The men turned away and went toward Sodom, but Abraham remained standing before the LORD.*

Jesus sent his two angels to look over Sodom and Gomorrah, and he stayed and talked with Abraham. At this point, Abraham begins begging Jesus to save the city. In reality, the best thing for Abraham to achieve the promise God had for him would be to have this wicked, sinful city destroyed. So why is he begging God to save it? The answer is found in Genesis 19:1.

> *The two angels arrived at Sodom in the evening, and Lot was sitting in the gateway of the city.*

Lot had moved into Sodom! He had originally picked land in the area of this wicked city. He had lived on the outskirts of the city when he had been taken captive. Now, twenty-four years later, we find he and his family moved into the wicked city!

Abraham knew this, and out of love and concern for his nephew, he begs God to save the city, that, in reality, would have been best destroyed for his own good. But twenty-four years ago, he took Lot with him, and he was still suffering for this decision!

The decision to take Lot with him had long-lasting effects for Abraham. For twenty-four years, he was always having battles and struggles and issues. But the issue wasn't over. God rescued Lot and his two daughters from Sodom before he destroys it, but then we read that his daughters fear they will never marry. So they devise a plot to make sure they have heirs!

Lot and his two daughters left Zoar and settled in the mountains, for he was afraid to stay in Zoar. He and his two daughters lived in a cave. One day the older daughter said to the younger, "Our father is old, and there is no man around here to give us children—as is the custom all over the earth. Let's get our father to drink wine and then sleep with him and preserve our family line through our father."

That night they got their father to drink wine, and the older daughter went in and slept with him. He was not aware of it when she lay down or when she got up.

The next day the older daughter said to the younger, "Last night I slept with my father. Let's get him to drink wine again tonight, and you go in and sleep with him so we can preserve our family line through our father." So they got their father to drink wine that night also, and the younger daughter went in and slept with him. Again he was not aware of it when she lay down or when she got up.

So both of Lot's daughters became pregnant by their father. The older daughter had a son, and she named him Moab; he is the father of the Moabites of today. The younger daughter also had a son, and she named him Ben-Ammi; he is the father of the Ammonites of today.

You may be thinking, "What a horrible story, but what does it have to do with Abraham?"

Well, the answer is this. Fast-forward a few hundred years to the book of Judges. Abraham's children have become God's chosen people, freed from slavery in Egypt. They now live in the Promised Land. You know who they have to constantly fight and try and live free from bondage of? The Moabites and Ammonites! Hundreds of years later, Abraham's children are struggling with Lot's children. Why? Because Abraham took Lot with him!

Guys, Abraham was called by God to a new way of life, full of promises and blessings. All Abraham had to do was leave his old way of life and follow God.

Abraham did this. However, he took one person from his past with him, and he suffered for generations because of it. We need to learn from his story and make sure we don't make the same mistakes.

> **Your "Lot" is anything from your past or your old way of life that keeps you from wholehearted surrender and abandonment to God and where he is leading you.**

I don't know what your "Lot" is in your life.

It could be a relationship.

It could be a sinful behavior.

It could be an addiction.

Your "Lot" is anything that is anything from your past or your old way of life that keeps you from wholehearted surrender to God and where he is leading you. I know in my life I had a few "Lots" I had to deal with.

I had friendships that were unhealthy and keeping me from becoming wholeheartedly devoted to God. I had to end these friendships so they didn't keep trying to bog me down and keep me in my old way of life.

I had thought patterns and mindsets that kept me from flourishing for God. I had to reprogram my way of thinking and acting and allow God to transform my mind.

I had areas of bondage such as pornography, unforgiveness, and rage that couldn't come with me on the journey God called me to as I grow spiritually. These are just some of the "Lots" that couldn't come with me. I had to leave them behind so they didn't constantly trip me up going forward with God.

I had to once and for all leave my "Lots" behind me.

I had to repent to God for these sins.

I spent time with the Holy Spirit, allowing him to show me how these sins affected me.

I analyzed how they got into my life in the first place. What compromises had I committed? What needs in my life did these fill in me that I should have been getting filled by God?

I made lists. I repented of sins. I removed influences in my life that opened the door for me to sin. There were relationships I had to end that were having negative influences on me. There were activities and hobbies I had to abandon that contributed to my sins. I had to leave anything and everything behind that was keeping me bound to my old life and patterns. Lot couldn't come with me!

What about you? What are your "Lots"? Are there relationships that are causing you to sin or stay in your old way of life? Do friendships have to end for you to follow God wholeheartedly?

Are there things from your old, carnal way of life that you have brought with you into the new life in Christ that God has given to you? Sins, habits, bondages? If so, what are they?

Ask the Holy Spirit to reveal them to you so that you can identify them, look them in the eye, and say, "You can't come with me! I am going forward with Christ and I am leaving you behind!"

Only then can you truly experience everything that God has for your life! The only way to excel in your walk with God is leaving your old life behind. Will you commit to doing this?

Dear heavenly Father, I come to you today as a man committed to following you wholeheartedly. In order to do this, I need to identify and remove my "Lot." Father, you know my relationship with _____ has been affecting my walk with you and has been dragging me back to my old way of life. But I am committed to going forward with you; help me to have the strength to end this relationship.

Father, you know I have been stuck in the bondage of _____. Please help me to overcome. This bondage can't come with me for one more day! Set me free, In Jesus' name, amen!

TRAINING DRILL

We discussed the need to leave old relationships and friendships behind that are influencing us in a negative way. Ask a trusted mentor or family mentor if he sees any such relationships in your life. Then, as painful as it may be, walk away from these relationships. Pray for these friends, but limit your interaction with them.

TWO-A-DAYS

Join a small group at your church. You need to develop relationships with like-minded believers who can help you in your walk with God. No man is an island, and we need to surround ourselves with fellow believers.

TEAM MEETING

1. What is your "Lot," or the thing from your past that you struggle to leave behind you?

2. How can you leave your negative relationships behind while still reflecting the love of Jesus to these people?

3. Who do you enjoy spending time with, fellow believers or unbelievers?

4. What sins or bondages from your past do you struggle to overcome?

5. What stands out to you the most about Abraham's story? What did you learn from studying his game footage to help you avoid the trap he fell into in his life?

6. How can we as a group help you?

CHAPTER 5

PLAYING BY THE RULES

Recently I was in my car on another long road trip. As I drove, I flipped my radio to a sports talk show to help pass the time. On this particular day, the show was discussing a legendary linebacker who had recently retired. The reason they were talking about him was because this player, who played his entire career completely bald—I mean no-hair-at-all bald—had recently been seen with a full head of hair.

The sportscasters were making various comments about the new hairdo, which was obviously plugs, and one point they made over and over was that this player wouldn't have been nearly as intimidating on the football field if he had this new look instead of the bald head he had when he played. It was a funny conversation. Everyone knew his hair, or lack of it, had nothing to do with the way he played the game or the passion to win he had on the inside. Yet, after viewing his picture when I got home, I have to admit, his outward appearance really did look less intimidating, and part of me wondered if it really would have affected his play.

This conversation reminded me of a man in the Bible whose accomplishments for God were closely tied to his hair. One of the most interesting stories in the Bible appears to revolve around a man's hairstyle, but like the athlete listed above, it really wasn't about the hair. As we look at the life of Samson, we will see that while his long flowing mane was front and center in the story, the real problem was the level of devotion he had for God.

Samson could have been known as the greatest man in the Old Testament, but he continuously chose to disobey God, all because his inner man was not anything like the image he tried to present to people. Let's look at his story in the book of Judges to see what I mean.

Samson lived during the time of the judges. This was a rocky time for the nation of Israel as they found themselves stuck in a destructive cycle.

Joshua, their leader, died, and they were left to serve God on their own. However, the people refused to stay faithful to God and began to worship the false gods around them. As a result, God would send an enemy to attack and oppress them. The people would cry out to God for deliverance, and he would send a judge—a deliverer—to rescue them. Once free, the people would once again turn on God, and the second verse was the same as the first as the mad cycle went on and on.

Samson's life was unique. For starters, his conception was announced by Jesus Christ himself.

Judges 13:2–5 says, *"A certain man of Zorah, named Manoah, from the clan of the Danites, had a wife who was childless, unable to give birth. The angel of the* LORD *[Jesus] appeared to her and said, 'You are barren and childless, but you are going to become pregnant and give birth to a son. Now see to it that you drink no wine or other fermented drink and that you do not eat anything unclean. You will become pregnant and have a son whose head is never to be touched by a razor because the boy is to be a Nazirite, dedicated to God from the womb. He will take the lead in delivering Israel from the hands of the Philistines.'"*

When Samson was born, his parents were faithful to raise him as a Nazarite, and, when he was grown, he would become a judge in Israel. To completely understand the story of Samson, you need to understand what it means to be a Nazarite.

In the Hebrew Bible, a Nazarite refers to one who took a vow described in Numbers 6:1–21. The term *Nazarite* comes from the Hebrew word *nazir*, meaning "consecrated" or "separated." This vow required the man or woman to:

- Abstain from wine, wine vinegar, grapes, raisins, and alcohol.
- Refrain from cutting the hair on one's head.
- Avoid corpses and graves, even those of family members, and any structure which contains such things.

Although most people took this vow for a specific period of time, Samson was to be a Nazarite for his entire life. His parents were both committed to keeping their promise to God; however, Samson's heart was not committed to God. His attitude was, "What they don't know won't hurt them." As long as everything appeared to be right in his life, he didn't care if he really was keeping his covenant with God. He only cared if he looked like he was on the team playing by God's rules; he didn't actually care if he was in the game. We get our first example of this in Judges 14.

Samson was all grown up and looking for a wife. However, he had little interest in Israelite women. Samson liked foreign women. However, God clearly instructed the Israelites not to marry foreigners.

Samson didn't care what God wanted—he wanted what he wanted. Soon, Samson told his mom and dad about the foreign woman he wanted to marry. Together, they went to meet her.

While they were on their way to her town, Samson had an interesting adventure.

Samson went down to Timnah together with his father and mother. As they approached the vineyards of Timnah, suddenly a young

*lion came roaring toward him. The Spirit of the LORD came pow-
erfully upon him so that he tore the lion apart with his bare hands
as he might have torn a young goat. But he told neither his father
nor his mother what he had done. Then he went down and talked
with the woman, and he liked her.*

*Some time later, when he went back to marry her, he turned aside
to look at the lion's carcass, and in it he saw a swarm of bees and
some honey. He scooped out the honey with his hands and ate as
he went along. When he rejoined his parents, he gave them some,
and they too ate it. But he did not tell them that he had taken the
honey from the lion's carcass.*

Hold it! First of all, gag me! How disgusting! He ate honey from
the stomach of a rotting animal's corpse.

Secondly, it says he was alone in a vineyard when this happened.
As a Nazarite, a vineyard was a no-no, no grapes or grape products allowed!

Third, isn't one of the Nazarite requirements that you not touch
anything that is dead?

You certainly aren't supposed to be eating honey from dead animals!

This incident gives insight into Samson's heart. Personally, he had
very little regard for his Nazarite vows. We see here he broke two of the
three requirements of the Nazarite vow.

The two he broke were inward things, things people couldn't see.
He still appeared to be in the game. To everyone around him, Samson
with his long hair looked to be a good Nazarite.

But he had no respect for this vow. What he did have was a knack
for deceiving his parents who wanted him to keep his vow! To avoid
this problem, he just didn't tell them where he got the honey. After all,
what they don't know won't hurt them. As long as everything looks

good, it is good. But in reality, Samson's walk with God was a mess. Outwardly he looked good, but inside he was a mess!

Samson went on to become engaged to this Philistine woman. As they prepared for the wedding, Samson decided to get cute with the Philistines.

Samson held a feast, as was customary for young men.

When the people saw him, they chose thirty men to be his companions.

"Let me tell you a riddle," Samson said to them. "If you can give me the answer within the seven days of the feast, I will give you thirty linen garments and thirty sets of clothes. If you can't tell me the answer, you must give me thirty linen garments and thirty sets of clothes."

"Tell us your riddle," they said. "Let's hear it." He replied, "Out of the eater, something to eat; out of the strong, something sweet."

Okay, this is wrong on so many levels. First of all, he was supposed to be Israel's redeemer from the Philistine oppression, yet here he was palling around with them. It's like playing against a team in a best-of-seven series, but between games going to dinner with the other team. He had no business hanging with them!

Second, his riddle is all based on the sin he had just committed against God! He broke his Nazarite vow, and now he was making a joke out of it.

Samson didn't take his relationship with God or the call on his life seriously at all. He liked the benefits that went with it, the glory, the fame, the reverence, but he didn't want to walk the walk as he went around talking the talk. He looked good on the outside, his flowing mane distinguished him as a devoted Nazarite, but inside he had little regard for the call of God.

Back to the story.

The men couldn't figure out Samson's riddle, so they bullied his fiancée into making Samson tell her the answer.

Samson told her the answer, she told the men, and the men told Samson.

Now Samson owed them thirty new outfits. Angry at losing the bet, Samson sprung into action.

Then the Spirit of the LORD *came powerfully upon him. He went down to Ashkelon, struck down thirty of their men, stripped them of everything and gave their clothes to those who had explained the riddle. Burning with anger, he returned to his father's home. And Samson's wife was given to one of his companions who had attended him at the feast.*

For the first time in this passage, we see Samson in action. The dude was a beast! Think the Hulk in his right mind and without the green issues. The Philistines definitely didn't like him when he got angry! He went and dealt a blow to Israel's enemy. However, while he did what God called him to do, he was doing it for the wrong reasons! It wasn't out of devotion to God or loyalty to his nation, it was out of spite from losing a bet. Still, to those looking on who didn't know the backstory, it looked like the long-haired Nazarite was defending his nation, an image Samson was happy to live with. He outwardly looked like he was playing by the rules; who cares if he really was or not? What they didn't know wouldn't hurt them, and it sure would help him!

Samson won a victory over the Philistines, but it came at a cost. His fiancée was given to another man. Samson once again sought revenge, and as a result his fiancée died.

Samson was really angry now. He took revenge, and because of this, the Philistines gave the Israelites an ultimatum: hand over Samson or die!

Samson agreed to be turned over to Philistines, but once they took him away from the city, he let his inner Hulk roar!

They bound him with two new ropes and led him up from the rock. As he approached Lehi, the Philistines came toward him shouting. The Spirit of the LORD came powerfully upon him. The ropes on his arms became like charred flax, and the bindings dropped from his hands. Finding a fresh jawbone of a donkey, he grabbed it and struck down a thousand men.

Samson dealt a devastating blow to the Philistines. It looked like Samson finally was fulfilling his call as the Nazarite judge. However, we can't ignore one minor detail in this passage.

Finding a fresh jawbone of a donkey, he grabbed it and struck down a thousand men.

Once again, Samson chooses to break the Nazarite vow. He wasn't supposed to mess with dead carcasses. However, instead of trusting in God's protection and help, he turns to his own methods, abandoning the requirements of God. Sure, he got the victory, but at the price of being unfaithful to God.

Then Samson said, "With a donkey's jawbone I have made donkeys of them. With a donkey's jawbone I have killed a thousand men."

The passage makes it clear that the Holy Spirit filled Samson and that is how he got the victory. But Samson was so far from God and had bought into so much of his own press that he didn't give God any glory. He took it all for himself. He was so far from the man he appeared to be!

Guys, we can't be men like Samson. It is a trap that unfortunately a lot of men in the church fall into. They don't have a genuine personal commitment to following God and God's ways. Sure, Samson enjoyed the benefits of God's blessing on his life. He reveled in the blessings. However, he never realized the source of his strength came from God. There was no attitude of humility or gratefulness to God for giving him his incredible abilities. Rather, Samson became conceited, arrogant and full of himself. He became cocky and saw himself as invincible. He felt it was safe to mess around with sin and compromise. Without a heart-felt commitment to God, it was easy for Samson to take his God-given abilities for granted, and fall prey to his enemies. While it all looked good to the casual onlooker, his walk with God was not what people thought it was. He looked good on the outside, but that was about to change.

> **Samson became conceited, arrogant and full of himself. He became cocky and saw himself as invincible. He felt it was safe to mess around with sin and compromise. Without a heart-felt commitment to God, it was easy for Samson to take his God-given abilities for granted, and fall prey to his enemies.**

Most of us know the story of Samson and Delilah. She was a Philistine with whom Samson was completely smitten. That sentence alone gives us keen insight into the state of Samson's heart.

Think about it: he was Israel's judge and leader. What was he doing with a Philistine, who was more than likely a prostitute?

Obviously, he was blatantly disobeying God's Law and sinning sexually. But think about the arrogance in Samson's life: he was openly sleeping with the enemy. His calling in life was to defeat the Philistines. Instead, Samson has fallen in love with a Philistine! What was he thinking?

Soon the game between Samson and Delilah began. (A game he had no business even playing!)

So Delilah said to Samson, "Tell me the secret of your great strength and how you can be tied up and subdued."

Samson answered her, "If anyone ties me with seven fresh bow-strings that have not been dried, I'll become as weak as any other man."

Samson lied, and she believed the lie. Delilah told her people and they tried to capture him. Because Samson lied, they were unsuccessful. Needless to say, Delilah was not happy. Again, she went to Samson and again he lied and escaped.

Delilah was not to be deterred. Instead of leaving her altogether and doing the job God called him to do, Samson continued to play around with his spiritual life. His arrogance led him to be more brazen.

Delilah then said to Samson, "All this time you have been making a fool of me and lying to me. Tell me how you can be tied."

He replied, "If you weave the seven braids of my head into the fabric on the loom and tighten it with the pin, I'll become as weak as any other man." So while he was sleeping, Delilah took the seven braids of his head, wove them into the fabric and tightened it with the pin.

Again she called to him, "Samson, the Philistines are upon you!" He awoke from his sleep and pulled up the pin and the loom, with the fabric.

Samson was getting awfully close to the line here! He had long ago abandoned his walk with God, but he never went so far as to cross the line and make his outward appearance match his inward appearance.

This lie had a direct tie to the final outward strand of his vow, his hair. However, he had long ago abandoned the vow; he just still wanted to look good. Nothing bad had happened from the other times he broke the vow, why would this be different?

Finally, Delilah had enough. In a last-ditch effort, she had "the talk" with Samson.

Then she said to him, "How can you say, 'I love you,' when you won't confide in me? This is the third time you have made a fool of me and haven't told me the secret of your great strength." With such nagging she prodded him day after day until he was sick to death of it.

So he told her everything. "No razor has ever been used on my head," he said, "because I have been a Nazarite dedicated to God from my mother's womb. If my head were shaved, my strength would leave me, and I would become as weak as any other man."

When Delilah saw that he had told her everything, she sent word to the rulers of the Philistines, "Come back once more; he has told me everything." So the rulers of the Philistines returned with the silver in their hands. After putting him to sleep on her lap, she called for someone to shave off the seven braids of his hair, and so began to subdue him. And his strength left him.

Then she called, "Samson, the Philistines are upon you!" He awoke from his sleep and thought, "I'll go out as before and shake myself free." But he did not know that the LORD had left him.

Sometimes when I read these verses I think, "Why was Samson so stupid? Why couldn't he see what Delilah was doing? Why did he tell her his secret? Didn't he know that she would cut his hair? Honestly, how dumb was he?"

I believe the answer isn't that he was dumb, but he was deceived.

Because he didn't have his own personal relationship with God and commitment to God, Samson took God's blessing on his life for granted. He began relying on his own strength and became full of himself. While his original attitude was to make sure things looked good on the outside, his arrogance eventually led to his not caring how it looked. He'd been disobeying and disregarding God's laws for years without any consequences. Would it really matter if he cut his hair? Wouldn't he still be Samson, the strongest man in the world? Did he really need God? Did it really matter if he followed God's rules?

Honestly, I don't think anyone was more surprised than Samson when he woke up and his strength was gone. Samson played with God's laws and tried to push the limits of God's boundaries all of his life. He never took his calling or his commitment to God seriously. When he finally stepped over the line, he wasn't repentant or even aware he'd done anything wrong. He didn't even know God had left him. He thought because he was Samson he could get away with anything. He played a dangerous game, which he eventually lost.

The Philistines came and captured him, gouged out his eyes, and put him in shackles in prison. Because he was only playing games with God and appearing to follow him, Samson's sin and heart problems ultimately destroyed him.

You have to understand, it wasn't the actual haircut that did him in—it was the attitude behind the haircut. His choices to only outwardly look like a man of God while ignoring the inner part led him to eventually become deceived and think he was invincible no matter what he did. Guys, we have to learn from Samson's life and not repeat his mistakes.

> **We need to make sure that we do more than just look like a follower of God; we actually have to follow! We can't act like Satan as long as we look like Jesus.**

We need to make sure that we do more than just look like a follower of God; we actually have to follow!

We can't act like Satan as long as we look like Jesus.

The Bible is clear: outward appearance doesn't matter; what matters is what's inside, a heart of love and devotion to God, a heart that would do whatever God ask, no matter the cost.

Instead of sacrificing his sinful nature to become the man God wanted him to be, Samson sacrificed God's blessing on his life for the things he wanted. He continually dropped the ball, and eventually it cost him, big time. He lost his eyesight, his strength, and his freedom.

Guys, this is a serious thing we are talking about here. I firmly believe God has had enough of men who are Christians in name only, men who go to church on Sunday and the live like everyone else the rest of the week.

The call to be a godly man is not a two-hours-a-week call, it is a twenty-four-hours-a-day, seven-days-a-week, 365-days-a-year call for all eternity.

Eventually, like Samson, a man who is a Christian in name only will be exposed. That is the bad news. However, there is good news. There is hope.

You see, we can change at any time! We can commit to become the man of God inwardly that everyone sees outwardly. Redemption can happen. It did with Samson!

Then the Philistines seized him, gouged out his eyes and took him down to Gaza. Binding him with bronze shackles, they set him to grinding grain in the prison. But the hair on his head began to grow again after it had been shaved.

Samson's hair began to grow again. Remember, it wasn't about the hair. It was about the character inside. I believe Samson's humiliation caused him to re-evaluate his life and his choices. I think he had a God-moment in this prison. I think his pride was broken as he saw that he really was nothing, God was everything. In my opinion, his hair growing was the outward sign of an inward change.

Now the rulers of the Philistines assembled to offer a great sacrifice to Dagon their god and to celebrate, saying, "Our god has delivered Samson, our enemy, into our hands."...While they were in high spirits, they shouted, "Bring out Samson to entertain us." So they called Samson out of the prison, and he performed for them.

When they stood him among the pillars, Samson said to the servant who held his hand, "Put me where I can feel the pillars that support the temple, so that I may lean against them." Now the temple was crowded with men and women; all the rulers of the Philistines were there, and on the roof were about three thousand men and women watching Samson perform. Then Samson prayed to the LORD, "Sovereign LORD, remember me. Please, God, strengthen me just once more, and let me with one blow get revenge on the Philistines for my two eyes."

Samson finally got it! This is the first time we read of Samson recognizing his strength came from God. He now knew he needed God, not the other way around. He worked for God, God didn't work for him. Yes, his hair grew back, but inside, his heart had changed as well. His inward man finally matched his outward appearance. He was God's man, inside and out.

Then Samson reached toward the two central pillars on which the temple stood. Bracing himself against them, his right hand on the one and his left hand on the other, Samson said, "Let me die with the Philistines!" Then he pushed with all his might, and down came the temple on the rulers and all the people in it. Thus he killed many more when he died than while he lived.

Samson's greatest accomplishment for God's kingdom came when he did it God's way and through God's strength. He had to learn the lesson the hard way, but at least he finally learned it. Lucky for us, we don't have to learn it the hard way if we are willing to learn from Samson's game tape.

What lesson are we suppose to learn from Samson?

The lesson is this. Our inside life needs to match our outward appearance. Unfortunately, many churchs have men following Samson's example. They know God's laws. They even teach God's laws. They just don't live according to God's laws.

For instance, I knew a man who taught other people about the need to live on a budget and manage their money properly. However, he felt like he was a special case, so he didn't apply these principles to his own life. Of course, the result was financial disaster.

Other men are so arrogant that they feel they could never fall into sexual sin. They push the boundaries and allow themselves to participate in activities with women who are not their wives. Some men feel it's okay to flirt with other women as long as it doesn't go any further.

> **God doesn't have special people who get special rules. Believing rules don't apply to you is simply a way of rationalizing away sin. Like Samson, living with this attitude will ultimately destroy you.**

Again, because of their arrogance and their perception that rules don't apply to them, they are usually trapped and destroyed by sin.

These are just a few examples. Arrogance can shine through in all areas of our lives.

The truth is that God's laws apply to all of us. God doesn't have special people who get special rules. Believing rules don't apply to you is simply a way of rationalizing away sin. Like Samson, living with this attitude will ultimately destroy you.

We need to strive to be men who are the same person no matter who we are with or what we are doing. You can't be a deceitful man who presents himself as a good Christian, good husband, good worker, and good father to the world, but lives like a completely different person behind closed doors.

Here are a few questions we all can ask ourselves:

- Do I obey God's rules for living out of a heart of love and gratitude to God, or do I see God's rules for living as a hassle?

Samson had no regard for God's rules for him, and he rejected them every chance he got.

- Do I try to stretch the boundaries as far as I can without getting caught?

Samson looked good outwardly, but he always was getting as close to the line as possible. What about you?

- Do I prefer to spend my time with non-Christians or fellow believers?

Almost all of Samson's story shows him hanging around with the Philistines, not his own Israelite people. Who do you spend time with?

- Do my friends build me up spiritually and support my faith or do I prefer to be with people who disregard God's ways?

Samson spent most of his time with Philistines who constantly got him to do things that went against God's call on his life.

- What do you do when you sin?

Although we rarely think about this, how we respond to sin gives keen insight into our hearts. Let's be real. We all sin sometimes. Knowingly or unknowingly, we all hurt other people. As long as we are human, we will all struggle with sin. What's important is how we respond to sin. How do you respond when the Holy Spirit convicts you of sin or someone confronts you with sin in your life?

- Are you defensive?
- Do you make excuses or play it down like it's no big deal?
- Do you become angry? Do you deny it happened?
- Are you repentant? Are you truly sorry for the wrong you have done?

- Do you express sorrow for your sin? Do you ask God and everyone that was hurt to forgive you?
- Are you willing to talk about what happened and work through issues or do you wonder why everyone is making such a big deal?
- Do you make every effort to completely change your behavior?

The answers to these questions are *so* important. They reveal what is inside of a person's heart.

Samson repeatedly broke God's laws, yet he never felt the need to repent or try to change. Will you be remembered for the same, or will you commit to not just looking like a Christian, but living like one too?

It's time for God's men to not just talk the talk, but to walk the walk. Samson had to lose it all to realize this and do things God's way. What will you do? It's decision time, before it is too late!

Dear heavenly Father, Please forgive me for any time I have arrogantly thought I could live however I want. Forgive me for any hypocrisy on my part as I tried to present one image while inside I am completely different.

Father, I want to be a genuine follower of you. I know this means living by your rules and standards in all areas of my life. I commit myself to this today. I don't want to be like Samson, I want to be like Jesus. Help me as I move forward. In Jesus' name, amen!

TRAINING DRILL

1. At the end of this chapter we listed some reflective questions. Honestly answer each question. Take time with the Holy Spirit and allow him to show you areas of your life that need to change based on your answers.

2. Ask a trusted friend or mentor how he would answer those questions for you. Don't be defensive with his reply, instead honestly accept his feedback and take his advice on ways to change.

TWO-A-DAYS

One of Samson's biggest weakness was he consistently spent his time with bad influences instead of with his fellow Israelites. Commit to developing relationships with other believers. Join a small group at your church and begin doing life with other believers.

TEAM MEETING

1. Have you ever struggled with feeling like God's rules are a hassle?

2. What do you do when you feel this way?

3. Who is your support system in life, believers or unbelievers?

4. Who do you prefer to spend your time with?

5. What stands out to you the most about Samson's story? What did you learn from studying his game footage to help you avoid the trap he fell into in his life?

6. How can we as a group help you?

PART 3 MOMENTUM KILLERS

PART 3
MOMENTUM
KILLERS

CHAPTER 6

NO PAIN, NO GAIN

At the 2016 Summer Olympic Games, the world watched as the U.S. women's gymnastics team dominated the rest of the world. Led by Aly Raisman and Simone Biles, our powerhouse team won the gold medal in the team event—by a lot!

They followed up their dominant team gold medal in the women's individual all-around, where Simone Biles and Aly Raisman won gold and silver, respectively. Honestly, our other gymnasts probably could have won bronze and fourth if not for a rule that each country can only have two women in the all-around—our team was that good.

U.S. women continued to dominate the individual events, concluding with the floor exercise where again Simone Biles and Aly Raisman won gold and silver. After this event, I watched Bob Costas interview these two amazing athletes. You would think the interview would focus on their skill and dominance. But these two athletes wanted to discuss only two things: meeting their heartthrob crush, Zac Efron, and finally being able to eat whatever they want!

They talked about eating cupcakes immediately after the final event. They playfully argued over who scarfed down the most french fries when their competition ended. They were excited about the next event after the interview, going out for pizza with Zac Efron. I don't know which they were more excited about, him or the pizza.

I have to be honest, I was embarrassed to admit I had eaten each of the items they were talking about in the past week. But hey, I am not a world-class athlete like they are. They knew they needed to say no to their appetites in order to train properly and compete at a top level.

As world-class athletes, they knew that, while in training, they had to say bye-bye to pizza and eat healthy foods like vegetables. They had to use self-control and not give into their cravings and urges. Many world-class athletes go cold turkey on all meat (pun intended), living the vegetarian lifestyle. I couldn't imagine being that dedicated to a sport that I would become a vegetarian. I am what you call a second-hand vegetarian—cows eat grass, and I eat cows.

Now if you're a vegetarian, don't quit reading this book! I respect your dedication to living healthier and avoiding meat. You have way more will power than I do.

I love steaks! I am a meat-and-potatoes guy. A good burger is heaven on earth to me. I enjoy a delicious pot roast or beef stew. I am in love with the candy of meats: bacon. I personally can't imagine life without bacon! I better move on, it is getting close to lunch and this discussion is making me hungry!

As much as I enjoy a juicy steak or a charbroiled burger, I wouldn't sacrifice all I had to get it. If my physical health demanded me to stop eating meat, I could do it. If my ability to serve God was inhibited by meat, I'd go cold turkey (Wait, that's still meat). If someone gave me the option of all God's promises being fulfilled, or a juicy porterhouse steak, no thought would be required. Anyone would choose God's blessings, right?

Wrong. Believe it or not, there is a man in the Bible who was such a fan of meat that he traded an amazing promise of God for a bowl of hearty stew! In reality, what he really was a fan of was instant gratification. You know, "I want what I want and I want it now, no matter the cost!"

Insisting on instant gratification is a dangerous attitude. Left unchecked, it can cause a great deal of sin and separation in our lives. It will devastate anyone who falls prey to its enticements.

Instant gratification is the natural enemy of any man who decides to get in the game. The athletes who make it in sports are the ones who lay aside instant gratification.

They get up early and stay late training.

They do without a social life in order to excel on the field.

They avoid shortcuts and illegal enhancements.

They can't live on bacon or cheeseburgers.

They know that, to excel in sports, they have to deny their selfish desires, their weaknesses, and their need to have what they want when they want it, and commit to a life of hard work and perseverance.

One thing is for sure—too many athletes who fumbled the ball did so because they gave in to instant gratification. The great ones, the ones who make it to their sports Hall of Fame, were men who refused to lose, and they refused to give in to instant gratification.

The same is true in our walk with God. In this chapter, we will examine Esau, a man who threw away the greatest promise in the Bible in order to get what he wanted. Esau demonstrates how costly it can be to seek instant gratification for our desires. He shows us why it is important to see the big picture and pursue all God has for us.

We find Esau's story in the book of Genesis. Esau was the oldest son of Isaac, and the grandson of Abraham. You know Abraham, the guy with the world's greatest promise of blessing on his life and lineage, the father of the nation of Israel.

Esau was next in line to receive the blessings God promised to his grandfather, namely, to be God's chosen people. This blessing also supplied great wealth, ownership of the Promised Land, and the distinction of having the Messiah come from his descendants.

As the oldest of Isaac's children, Esau was in line to inherit this amazing promise of God's blessing and protection on his life. He would be a wealthy and powerful man. He was born with the world at his feet. Unfortunately, there were other things he valued more than God's will for his life.

Esau was a rugged man. He loved hunting. He was an outdoorsy guy. Picture *Duck Dynasty*'s Jase Robertson. He was an outdoorsman supreme! He even looked the part, because Genesis describes him as hairy and smelly. Nothing was more enjoyable to Esau than the thrill of the hunt. It is no wonder that the passage we are going to study starts with Esau returning from a hunting expedition. Genesis 25:29–30:

> *Once when Jacob was cooking some stew, Esau came in from the open country, famished. He said to Jacob, "Quick, let me have some of that red stew! I'm famished!" (That is why he was also called Edom.)*

Esau wanted his younger twin brother, Jacob, to give him some of the food he had prepared. Jacob was the polar opposite of his older twin brother. He wasn't the rough-and-tumble man that Esau was. Jacob instead worked in the camp area.

On this particular day, Jacob cooked stew. Esau, who was exhausted and starved from his hunt, wanted Jacob's stew. He needed to fill his hungry belly. It was all he could think about!

Jacob, realizing the extreme hunger of Esau, used the situation to his advantage.

Jacob replied, "First sell me your birthright."

As the heir, Esau had most of the power and wealth. The heir received two-thirds of his father's possessions. He became the boss of the family, and everyone did what he said. As the younger of the two, Jacob was destined to a life of serving his older brother.

Jacob wanted Esau's inheritance for himself. He didn't want to be at his brother's mercy for the rest of his life. In a bold move, Jacob made an absurd demand: the family power and wealth, the very blessing of God, for a bowl of soup!

No one would take such a deal. Wrong!

"Look, I am about to die," Esau said. "What good is the birthright to me?" But Jacob said, "Swear to me first." So he swore an oath to him, selling his birthright to Jacob. Then Jacob gave Esau some bread and some lentil stew. He ate and drank, and then got up and left. So Esau despised his birthright.

Can you believe the stupidity of Esau?

He put the momentary desire for food ahead of a lifetime of blessing, wealth, and power. He couldn't see past the ache he felt in his stomach. Look again at what he said:

And Esau said, "Look, I am about to die; so what is this birthright to me?" (NKJV)

What a drama queen! Esau wasn't going to die of starvation. It was a thoughtless thing to say. Somewhere in the camp was food he could have eaten. However, he wanted the food in front of him so he could eat it right away. He put gratifying his own hunger before anything else. He made a stupid, short-sighted decision and it cost him everything!

Let's examine this deal Esau made. In exchange for some hot stew and a few lentils, Esau gave away the blessing of God, the wealth his father and grandfather had received from God, the land his father had accumulated, and the privilege of being the forefather of the future Messiah. Moses, the writer of Genesis, nailed it: Esau truly did despise his birthright! He placed the value of it so low that he gave it away to fill his stomach.

He could have had the world, but he chose to fulfill his immediate desires. Instant gratification was more important than the long-term blessing of God. Guys, we need to make sure we don't make the same mistake.

Let's face it. We live in a world where instant gratification is the norm. Microwaves and express lanes dominate. We get what we want when we want it. Instant gratification can lead us into dangerous sin if we aren't careful.

It can cause us to fall morally.

It can trap us in our business world.

It can destroy our family life.

It can ge a devastating sin that destroys everything in its path!

People fall into sin very easily when they think only about satisfying their desires.

One area where instant gratification is sinking men is financially. Instant gratification is leading many people into financial disaster.

They will pull a fast one to score a big business deal without considering how it could affect their reputation for the rest of their lives.

They have sex whenever they feel like it with whomever they want, not considering the destruction it brings to their families, relationships, and their own bodies.

Some party and drink in excess, not considering the effects it can have on their body and mind.

People smoke and do drugs, never thinking about the damage to their lungs and the rest of their body.

These are just a few of the sins people commit as they seek to get whatever they desire.

One area where instant gratification is sinking men is financially. Instant gratification is leading many people into financial disaster.

How? Well, we can get what we want when we want it, all courtesy of our little pieces of plastic. No pain of counting the money or having it on hand; swipe the card and all we want is ours.

This is *so* against God's will for our lives. God wants us whole-heartedly serving and following him. However, Proverbs says that debt makes us the servant of the lender. It keeps us from being able to fully serve God.

Still, many people buy things without having the means to pay for them. They don't stop and think ahead to what their future will be like as the bills grow larger and larger. They only see the things they want at the time. They are willing to do whatever is necessary to get them, even if it means paying hundreds of dollars extra in interest. Credit companies get richer and richer as we get more bound to debt. All because we have to have what we want now! Waiting and saving until we can afford it is rarely an option. We *need* it now! Debt lets us have it. All it costs us is our freedom.

People don't understand that debt will become their master. They will end up serving it. It can even keep them from serving God.

What if God asks them to go somewhere or do something for his kingdom and they have to say "no" because of all their debt? Obedience to God is sacrificed for paying off the debtors.

We need to get to the place where we think ahead and count the cost. We need to simplify our lives and meet our needs. The Bible says God will supply our needs, not our wants. We can't expect God to pay off our debt for extravagant wants. Debt has devastated many people, and much of it could be avoided by saying "no" to our desires and denying our need for instant gratification.

You may think this teaching is hard. Many people feel debt isn't really that big of a deal. However, I disagree.

I have experienced the consequences of living in debt. My father was the type of man who thought money was to be used to play and have fun. When money ran low, he would charge things. He kept the state of our finances a secret, so we didn't realize we were in trouble. However, we were. He had accumulated thousands of dollars in secret debt. He never told anyone. He just let it grow.

One day, my mom happened to open a letter. Inside she found the truth of my father's debt. We were devastated. He had been lying to us for years. Relationships were damaged. Trust was lost and lives were changed. We had to work really hard and cut back greatly. We did without in order to break free of our debt. We had to sell things. It was a rough few years.

We scrimped and saved, and eventually managed to get out of the huge financial mess my dad had made. He lived for the moment, gave no thought to the future, and used debt to finance it all. It was a money issue, but it resulted from the need for instant gratification.

This is why I feel so strongly on this subject. I have seen firsthand the destruction instant gratification leaves behind. It almost destroyed our family.

Instant gratification is a cruel taskmaster disguised as our best friend. It makes us feel it has our best interest at heart, and that it will help us get exactly what we deserve. But it does the exact opposite. It destroys us. It gives temporary satisfaction but leaves long-term devastation.

- Sexually, it fulfills our urges and desires temporarily, but interferes with and damages relationships all around us in the long term. Single guys, it will do just as much damage to your future wife as it does to married guys and their marriages.
- Financially, it gives us what we want now, but binds us up and takes away our long-term freedom and ability to obey God and serve him with complete abandon.
- Physically, we get the thrill and high of the moment, but long term we end up working harder and struggling more.

- Emotionally, we feel the short-term euphoria of getting exactly what we want when we want it, but long term we feel extreme stress when it comes time to pay the piper.
- Relationally, instant gratification will be an assassin. Sure, you will feel good temporarily, but those around you will suffer!

Think about it: three of the top causes of stress in relationships and divorce are marital infidelity, debt and money problems, and addiction. All three of these have instant gratification at the core. Divorce not only hurts the husband and wife, but damages parental relationships as kids are caught in the middle. Friendships get shattered and friends choose sides. Even churches suffer. Instant gratification destroys relationships, plain and simple.

Zig Ziglar once said, "Be careful not to compromise what you want most for what you want now."

Esau learned this lesson the hard way. His need for instant gratification cost him everything! God gave him the world and he traded it for a hot meal. Even the world's biggest meat fan would agree this was a bone-headed decision!

> **Zig Ziglar once said, "Be careful not to compromise what you want most for what you want now."**

Esau's decision to give up God's blessing to fill his stomach looks even dumber when you stop and compare it to another man in the Bible named Daniel.

Daniel lived during the time of Israel's history when the nation was under God's judgment. King Nebuchadnezzar conquered most of the Middle East, including the tribe of Judah to which Daniel belonged. As a member of the royal family of Judah, Daniel was chosen to be taken to Babylon to be indoctrinated into the Babylonian kingdom. He was a political prisoner at the mercy of the Babylonian king.

Once in Babylon, Daniel was immediately faced with a tough choice. Dinnertime came, and like Esau, food presented Daniel with a choice to either give in to or overcome instant gratification. Daniel 1:5–8,

> *The king assigned them a daily amount of food and wine from the king's table. …But Daniel resolved not to defile himself with the royal food and wine, and he asked the chief official for permission not to defile himself this way.*

Daniel could have gone for instant ease and peace by just editing the food put before him, but instead, he resisted the opportunity to advance himself in the Babylonian kingdom by rejecting God and his ways.

Instead, Daniel chose to take a stand and follow his God, and as a result, God gave him favor, and Daniel rose to become the second-most powerful man in the world, second only to Nebuchadnezzar.

Esau lost everything by seeking instant gratification; Daniel gained the world by rejecting the easy life of instant gratification by staying loyal to God. He wouldn't trade God's blessing for short-term satisfaction.

What about you?

What are you trading away to achieve instant gratification?

What is your pursuit of instant gratification stealing from you?

Guys, we need to examine ourselves. We can't be fully in the game if we are giving way to instant gratification. We need to ask ourselves some tough questions.

In the light of eternity, how have we given ground to instant gratification?

Are we trading God's long-term blessing for short-term satisfaction?

We need to all take this topic seriously.

We need to destroy our tendency toward pursuing instant gratification before it destroys us. We need to be men who pursue God's kingdom and will for our lives and sacrifice our wants and desires to do so.

It's the difference between being a champion or losing the game. What will you choose?

Dear heavenly Father, I want to be a man who is free to serve you in any way possible. I don't want to let anything get in the way of doing your will. Please forgive me for any time I sought to satisfy my own wants instead of seeking your will. I especially ask forgiveness for any debt I may have accumulated in order to get things I wanted and couldn't afford. Please give me wisdom to find a way to pay off all my debt as soon as possible. Give me the strength to stop spending until I am debt free.

I don't want to be a man who gives way to instant gratification any longer. Help me to plan for the future instead of always seeking to feel good in the present. I no longer want to serve my desires. I instead choose to serve you. In Jesus' name, amen.

TRAINING DRILL

We ended this chapter asking the question, "In light of eternity, how have we given ground to instant gratification?" Spend time with the Holy Spirit and allow him to show you areas in your life where you are entertaining instant gratification. Write them down. Then think through what the end result could be. Make changes to avoid these consequences.

TWO-A-DAYS

We discussed how debt is a form of instant gratification. Commit yourself to start getting out of debt. Read Dave Ramsey's *Total Money Makeover* and begin the process of getting control of your finances so your finances don't control you.

TEAM MEETING

1. In your own words, define *instant gratification.*

2. Instant gratification can take many shapes and forms. What areas do you struggle most with when it comes to instant gratification?

3. How is debt a form of instant gratification?

4. How did Daniel's choices differ from Esau's? What can we learn from these differences?

5. At the end of the chapter we asked, "Are we trading God's long-term blessing for short-term satisfaction?" What is your answer to this question?

6. What stands out to you the most about Esau's story? What did you learn from studying his game footage to help you avoid the trap he fell into in his life?

7. How can we as a group help you overcome?

CHAPTER 7

WINNERS NEVER CHEAT, AND CHEATERS NEVER WIN

Ever since I was a young boy, I have been a fan of the Philadelphia Phillies. I remember as a child making the two-hour drive to the Phillies old stadium, Veteran Stadium, to watch my heroes play a game, live and in person. The giant concrete stadium seemed so huge to my young eyes; you could see it from blocks away as you approached.

I remember how green the grass was on the field, it was so beautiful. I remember cheering my heart out as the Fightin' Phils took the field to begin the game. I recall cheering my guts out when my baseball hero, Mike Schmidt, came to bat, wishing and praying that he would either hit a home run, or at least hit a foul ball to me. Back in the day, the Phillies teams I saw had superstars on them. Mike Schmidt, Von Hayes, Gary Maddux, Steve Carlton, and, of course, the legendary Pete Rose.

Almost everyone, baseball fan or not, knows the name Pete Rose. To this day, his name is frequently in the news. However, Charlie Hustle, as he was known as a player, is not really remembered for his all-star hitting, defensive play, and general "all-in" hustle he exhibited on the field. If ever there was a man whose play on the field should have guaranteed him a spot in the Hall of Fame, it was Pete Rose. However, that is not his legacy.

Instead, this Hall of Fame-worthy slugger is known for breaking one of the cardinal rules of baseball—you don't bet on the games. Pete Rose bet on baseball games, including games his teams played in. He broke the sacred trust of the game, choosing to disobey the most basic of principles of fairness. As a result, he was and is still banned from baseball. Pete's disobedience cost him everything!

Pete Rose is not alone in his cheating scandals. Whether it be football players allegedly deflating footballs, NASCAR teams deflating tires, baseball players inflating muscles via steroids, or basketball refs betting on games, sports is not immune to people cheating to try and get ahead. However, they rarely do.

When you boil it down, cheating is for all intents and purposes lying and deceit. Deceit is destructive to an athlete. It is devastating to a man of God.

When I think of an example of a man who almost lost it all because of deceit, Jacob springs to my mind. Jacob's life proves that deceitfulness and lying can be devastating. It can destroy relationships and change lives forever. It will keep us from a truly intimate and close relationship with God. In this chapter, we will see how lying and deceit kept Jacob from fully experiencing the blessing of God. Instead, these sins opened him up to a lifetime of difficulty and sorrow when the lies started coming back to haunt him.

Jacob's story is found in Genesis chapters 25–37. Since his life is so involved, I will relate the story instead of citing the actual passage. If you think I am deceiving you, check it out for yourself.

Jacob was the younger of the twin sons. The Bible shows us in Genesis 26 that when Isaac, Jacob's father, would get in a pinch, he would use deceit to get out of it. Jacob learned his father's behavioral pattern of lying and deceit. It became his way of life whenever he faced difficulties. However, each time Jacob lied or practiced deceit, it ended up causing him hurt, pain, and loss.

The first time we read about Jacob's deceit is with his aging father. Before he died, Isaac deemed it his responsibility to give the promised birthright to his son, Esau. Earlier, we saw how Esau foolishly traded the birthright away, but apparently Isaac still planned on giving the blessing to Esau. He asked Esau to go get him some fresh game meat to eat before he blessed him. So Esau grabbed his camo gear and went a-hunting. Okay, the Bible doesn't actually say he wore camo, but it's how I picture it!

Meanwhile, Rebekah, Isaac's wife, overheard this conversation between her hubby and son, and she immediately told Jacob, aka the ultimate momma's boy, what was happening. Together, Rebekah and Jacob connived to trick Esau.

Rebekah's master plan was to have Jacob go to his practically blind, aging father and pretend to be Esau. It worked perfectly. Isaac gave Jacob the birthright. The plan went off without a hitch. They successfully took the inheritance away from Esau.

Jacob didn't wait on God to vindicate him and work things out on his behalf. He thought lies and deceit were enough to get him what he wanted. They got him the birthright, but would he be able to enjoy it? Not if Esau had anything to say about it!

Esau was furious! He became so angry with Jacob that he decided to kill him.

However, Rebekah found out about Esau's plan. Immediately, she sent Jacob away to live with her brother Laban.

Jacob escaped with his life, but his deceit cost him dearly. He had to leave his beloved mom and he never saw her again. She died before he returned. Their deceitful scheme together became the wedge that drove them apart. Deceit cost Jacob his closest relationship. He left home alone and broke.

Jacob went to live with his Uncle Laban. While living there, he fell in love with Rachel, Laban's daughter. He traded seven years of his life in hard labor to Laban for the privilege of marrying her. At the end of these years, Jacob's deceitful past came back full circle. He found himself on the receiving end of a con job orchestrated by Laban.

On the wedding night, Laban switched daughters on Jacob. He sent his oldest daughter, Leah, into Jacob's tent. Now, I have no idea why Jacob was so stupid not to realize she wasn't Rachel, but that's another topic for another time.

Leah was homely and unattractive, and her father figured the only way to marry her off was to trick someone into marrying her, and apparently he saw Jacob as the perfect mark to pull the scam on. Jacob was tricked into marrying the wrong girl. To marry Rachel, his real love, he was forced to work seven more years under Laban's heavy hand. The con man had been conned!

However, Jacob was not to be outdone. He returned to an old pattern of deceit to get what he wanted. Jacob went to Laban and told him he wanted to return home. He was tired of being poor and working for Laban. However, Laban would have none of it. Despite all of Jacob's lies, God hadn't given up on Jacob and was taking care of him. Laban was enjoying the fruit of this protection, and, if Jacob left, so did the blessing.

Instead of trusting God to provide for him and bless him, Jacob decided to do it himself. He devised a scheme to get rich. He used an old shepherd's trick to con Laban and make himself richer. Instead of trusting God to supply him with wealth, he used deceit to con Laban.

Laban's sons were outraged at the way Jacob duped their father. When Jacob heard of their anger, he packed up his family and ran away in the middle of the night. Once again Jacob's deceit cost him a place to call home.

Jacob spent his entire life practicing deceit. He never trusted God to take care of him. He didn't wait for God to vindicate him or work things out. He used deceit in much the same way his father had done. However, it never worked out.

As a matter of fact, it got worse. His deceitful ways were handed down to his sons. They learned from their dad how to lie and deceive to get what they wanted. Each time they followed their dad's behavioral patterns, they all lost something, especially Jacob.

Jacob's son's used deceit to get revenge on an entire city (Genesis 38). Again Jacob was forced to run away. This time the trip cost him his beloved wife Rachel, who was pregnant. She died in labor, exhausted from the hasty departure. Deceit took Jacob's mother, his wife, and any home he ever had. However, it didn't end there.

After the death of Rachel, Jacob turned all of his love and attention to Rachel's son, Joseph. He spoiled Joseph and made him the favorite son, causing his other sons to hate Joseph. They despised the favoritism and love he received from their father. Their hatred drove them to sell Joseph into slavery.

How did they tell Jacob the news about Joseph? They used their father's favorite method. They lied to their father about what they had done to Joseph.

They told Jacob that an animal had killed him. They even dipped Joseph's coat in blood as part of their lie.

Jacob, not knowing the truth, felt he had lost it all. Jacob's sons used lies and deceit, just like Jacob had done to Esau so many years ago. Deceit cost Jacob his mother, his wife, and now his son. Deceit never brings about a happy ending. Jacob learned this lesson the hard way.

Jacob's life would have been totally different if he had just trusted in God to do what he promised. The blessing of God was there for Jacob, but he never relied on God to help him. Instead, he used lies, deceit, manipulation, and conniving to get what he wanted. As a result, his life was marked by sin, pain, disappointment, and fear. He always lost more than he gained from his lies. Worse than that, he watched his sons throw their lives away, following his pattern of lies and deceit.

The Bible is very clear on God's feelings about lying and deceit. It is one of his Ten Commandments. He hates it!

Proverbs 12:22 (ESV) says, *"Lying lips are an abomination to the* LORD.*"*

That's a pretty strong statement about what God thinks of deceit and lying!

Lying is part of our sinful nature. When we practice lying and deceit, we are worshipping Satan, who is the father of lies. God's kingdom is built on perfect truth. He can have no part of deceit.

> **When we practice lying and deceit, we are worshipping Satan, who is the father of lies. God's kingdom is built on perfect truth. He can have no part of deceit.**

The Bible says that liars cannot get into heaven (Psalms 101:7, Revelation 21:8–9). As a matter of fact, the Revelation passage lists liars with the "big sinners"—murderers, the sexually immoral, witches, and idol worshippers. I'm pretty sure that means God has an issue with us lying and being deceitful. As you can see, nothing can be more devastating to our walk with God than lies and deceit.

Lies destroy relationships. Jacob's life is an excellent example of this truth. He was separated from his mother. It cost him his favorite wife and son. His relationship with Laban and his family was tumultuous because of deceit. He had a horrible relationship with his children who learned his ways and had no problem lying to his face.

Guys, we need to learn from Jacob's life. We need to learn from his game tape so we can overcome and win. We can't trade God's blessing for the quick benefits of lying and deceit.

We need to make sure we don't ever allow any deceit into our relationships. Lies destroy. They kill trust.

- Lying to your spouse will sink your marriage. If you're single, it will sink your relationship with your girlfriend.
- Lying to your boss could cost you your job.
- Lying to an employee will cause them to lose trust in you.
- Lying to your kids will cost you your relationship with them.

I know of what I speak. Being deceitful was a huge area of sin that the Holy Spirit pointed out in my life. The men in my family were very dishonest men. Lies and deceit were a common part of their lives.

Unfortunately, I became a man who picked up the family practice. Deceit became my default get-out-of-jail-free card. I use to be able to look someone right in the eyes and lie to them without blinking. It is one of my biggest areas of shame from my past, because it is an area where I lived in exact opposition to the nature of my heavenly Father.

The Holy Spirit began to show me I could never reach my full potential as a godly man as long as I continued to practice this pattern of lying and deceiving. I needed to change, and change now! God was so serious about breaking this sin engrained deep in me that he required that I only speak what was true. If I spoke anything that was not 100 percent accurate, I would have to go back and correct it. When I say anything, I mean ANYTHING! I was so zealous that I would correct the most minute details. I would correct statements, even if it was as simple as saying something "took me five minutes" and it actual took me six.

Once, the Holy Spirit reminded me of a time I lied while in college to avoid paying a fine. He required me to write the college a letter asking for forgiveness and include the money for the fine. It was hard to do, but I needed to break free of my natural tendency to lie. I wanted to be a man devoted to God. I wanted to experience the best things he had for me, and to serve him wholeheartedly. In order to do this, I had to destroy the natural tendency inside of me to lie.

God required me to remember times I had lied and go back and make things right when possible. For instance, once when I was about ten, I was playing with a relative and his friend. I really don't remember what happened (C'mon, it was twenty-eight years ago!) but they said something that really made me mad. In my anger, I swore at them, using a *really* filthy expletive.

Well, this relative went home and told his mom, who told my mom. I knew I was in huge trouble, so I lied to my mom and denied it. The result was a huge rift in the family. For years this part of our family refused to talk to us. They weren't believers, so my lie killed any witness to them. This went on for years, and I never told anyone the truth.

Then God started me on this process of destroying all deceit in my life. One of the first things he made me do was confess to my mom that I had lied so many years ago. Then he required me to humble myself, go to these relatives and ask them to forgive me for lying to them over ten years earlier. It was humiliating! But God asked me to do it, so I did it.

Let me tell you, this kind of action kills sin inside of you pretty quickly! With a lot of hard work, repentance, and humility, I was able to conquer and defeat this monstrous enemy of deceit that I had given a foothold in my life.

Guys, I cannot overemphasize the need for godly men to become honest men. We need to speak nothing but truth. Deceit can have no part in us.

There is no greater influence in our world than an example of honesty. The world is full of Jacobs. It is the norm to have people look you in the face and lie to you. It is an everyday event for employees to lie to both their bosses and their customers. The world doesn't blink when it is told a lie. However, it astonishes people when they meet an upright, honest man. It is a great way to be light in a dark world!

I remember once I was watching a golf tournament on TV. There was a young golfer named Brian Davis who was relatively unknown. However, he was in contention all weekend long at the Verizon Heritage PGA Tournament. When the tournament ended, he found himself in a tie for first place. It was time for a playoff and the chance at his first career win!

Davis's approach shot on the first hole of the playoff bounced off the green and nestled in among some weeds. When Davis tried to punch the ball up onto the green, his club grazed against a stray weed on his backswing. Davis knew that hitting any material around your ball during your backswing constitutes a violation of the rule against moving loose impediments, and is an immediate two-stroke penalty. In a playoff, that means, in effect, game over.

No one had noticed him grazing the weed; however, Brian knew it happened. He was faced with a decision: be deceitful and hide the mistake, or be honest and give up his first PGA event win.

Brian immediately called for a rules official and told them what happened. The infraction was unnoticeable to anyone unless you watched the video in slow motion, but Davis knew he did it, and he immediately told the truth, conceding the two strokes, and his first tournament victory. He gave away a chance at winning his first-ever PGA Tour event because he knew that in golf, as in life, honesty is more important than victory. He knew that winning is nothing without the integrity to go with it.

The funny thing is, if he had cheated and won, he would have won the tournament, but then the next week there would be a new winner, and the week after that, and over time, his victory would be forgotten. However, his act of integrity and honesty is still remembered and talked about today.

What a contrast to Jacob! Jacob chose to use lies and deceit to get what he wanted. He wasn't a man who trusted in God to take care of him and give him the life he was promised. We need to be different. We need to become men of truth, honesty, and justice.

We choose to be men who refuse to lose when we choose to walk in truth before God. So much can be gained from something so simple as telling the truth. No lie is worth what it costs. Jacob learned this lesson the hard way. We can avoid the same losses he endured. This can only be done as we daily speak absolute truth.

Dear heavenly Father, I am by nature a man given to lies and deceit. However, I want to serve you. I want to be delivered from my natural tendency to lie. I want to be a man who overcomes. I want to speak words of honesty and truth.

Father, please forgive me for every time I have lied. Forgive me for any time I used deceit, lies, and manipulation to get what I wanted in life. Help me to no longer follow in these patterns. Help me to be a man who trusts in you to take care of me. I want to become a man who leaves a legacy of honesty and truthfulness for the whole world to see. Help me as I try to become a man of integrity in a dishonest world. In Jesus' name, amen.

TRAINING DRILL

1. Start being hard on yourself. Whenever you say something that is not 100 percent true, immediately correct yourself and speak the truth. 2. Grab a concordance or do an online search to see what the Bible says about deceit and lying. As you read each verse, allow the Holy Spirit to convict you of lies you have told in the past. Spend time repenting of these lies, and ask God to change your heart so you only speak words of truth.

TWO-A-DAYS

In this chapter, we discussed times God made me go and apologize to others I had lied to in the past. Allow the Holy Spirit to show you people you have lied to, and humbly go and confess the sin to them and ask them to forgive you.

TEAM MEETING

1. How does deceit affect our relationship with God?

2. How does it affect our relationships with those around us?

3. How does it affect our witness to the lost?

4. How does God feel about deceit?

5. What stands out to you the most about Jacob's story? What did you learn from studying his game footage to help you avoid the trap he fell into in his life?

6. How can we as a group help you?

CHAPTER 8

WINNING AGAINST COMPROMISE

I knew it was wrong but I did it anyway. It happened when a buddy and I went golfing together. Because we were in college at the time, neither of us could afford to play an entire eighteen holes. Instead, we paid for nine. Both my friend and I played really well, and after our nine holes were over, we were tied. No guy wants to end anything tied! One of us had to win! (I am very competitive!!)

My friend suggested that we play one more hole to see who won. It was one of those times when you're faced with a small decision that helps shape your character. I knew we had only paid for nine holes and to go on was dishonest. However, I just had to win, so I went along with him and we started the tenth hole.

Of course, the club pro noticed that we kept playing. He got in a cart, and by the time we got to the green, had chased us down and demanded we immediately leave the course.

Because I compromised and did what I knew was wrong, we were embarrassed and forced to leave. Worse than that, we gave the club pro a terrible impression of the students at our college. We were horrible witnesses for Jesus on that day. It was made worse by the fact that I knew it was wrong but I went along with it anyway. I compromised, plain and simple.

By definition, *compromise* means "to accept standards that are lower than is desirable." The dictionary goes on to say it is a shameful or dishonorable concession, i.e., to compromise one's principles. Basically, it means to do something that is against our convictions. It's knowing something is wrong and doing it anyway.

Compromise is a touchy subject to address; however, we must look at it and face it. Compromising our beliefs is one of the easiest yet most dangerous things to do. It can affect our relationship with God in a greater way than any of the "big" sins. We need to study this topic so we can see the danger compromise poses to us as men seeking to grow and mature spiritually.

> **Compromising means to know something is wrong and choosing to do it anyway.**

In this chapter, we will examine the life of Solomon, one of the greatest kings in history. As we do, we will see how a few compromises ended up costing Solomon his throne. Instead of spiking the ball in the end zone, he scrambled to recover his fumble.

Solomon was the son of the great king of Israel, David. Solomon became the king of Israel when his father David was no longer physically able to do the job. He came to power with a mandate to build a temple for the Lord. It was David's dream and driving passion to build this temple, but the honor went to his son. It was a daunting task that faced Solomon, but he responded like a true, godly man. He sought God's face and asked him for the wisdom necessary to complete the task.

God was pleased with Solomon's request. He granted him not only wisdom, but power, wealth, and a promise that his descendants would always sit on the throne of Israel as long as Solomon obeyed him. Solomon was on his way to an MVP award. He had it all: wealth, the loyalty of his people, the respect of the surrounding nations, and the brains of Albert Einstein, Tony Stark, and Stephen Hawking combined!

Solomon's reign was off to a fabulous start. He led the great effort to build the temple. After a few years, he completed the mission that David his father had laid out for him. As we look at I Kings, we see God was impressed with both Solomon and his temple. In 1 Kings chapter 9, were see that he appeared to Solomon and gave him a tremendous promise.

> *"As for you, if you walk before me faithfully with integrity of heart and uprightness, as David your father did, and do all I command and observe my decrees and laws, I will establish your royal throne over Israel forever, as I promised David your father when I said, 'You shall never fail to have a successor on the throne of Israel.'"*

Jackpot! This was a tremendous promise from God. However, the promise had an alternative.

> *"But if you or your descendants turn away from me and do not observe the commands and decrees I have given you and go off to serve other gods and worship them, then I will cut off Israel from the land I have given them and will reject this temple I have consecrated for my Name. Israel will then become a byword and an object of ridicule among all peoples. This temple will become a heap of rubble. All who pass by will be appalled and will scoff and say, 'Why has the Lord done such a thing to this land and to this temple?' People will answer, 'Because they have forsaken the LORD their God, who brought their ancestors out of Egypt, and have embraced other gods, worshiping and serving them—that is why the LORD brought all this disaster on them.'"*

God didn't pull any punches with Solomon. There were no hidden strings or fine print. He laid it out plain and simple. God required obedience of Solomon. If he obeyed, he would be successful. However, his disobedience would mean the loss of God's blessing. It appears that Solomon took this warning seriously; for we read that he served God wholeheartedly for the early part of his life. As a result, he experienced God's blessings.

> *King Solomon was greater in riches and wisdom than all the other kings of the earth. The whole world sought audience with Solomon to hear the wisdom God had put in his heart. ...The king made silver as common in Jerusalem as stones, and cedar as plentiful as sycamore-fig trees in the foothills.*

Solomon experienced the blessings of God in a greater way than any man in history. He was smarter than everyone else, filthy rich, and, for probably the only time in all of Israel's history, had peace from all his enemies. Fat City!

Solomon was sitting in the lap of luxury. However, it didn't last.

Solomon fell into a trap that we all face. He began to make compromises. He started doing things he knew were wrong to do. They were little at first, but they ended up costing him big time.

Solomon's compromise began in the form of a peace treaty. He made a deal with the king of Egypt. He would marry the king's daughter in exchange for peace and trade agreements. While this seems like no big deal, we see in Deuteronomy 7 that it was a *huge* deal.

> *"Make no treaty with them, and show them no mercy. Do not intermarry with them. Do not give your daughters to their sons or take their daughters for your sons, for they will turn your children away from following me to serve other gods, and the LORD's anger will burn against you and will quickly destroy you."*

This treaty and marriage that Solomon agreed to was expressly forbidden by God. This was the first act that led Solomon into deeper sin.

His Egyptian wife was not a follower of God, so Solomon built her a place of her own away from the temple, just like the passage in Deuteronomy predicted would happen. It seemed like a small thing—marry a foreign leader's daughter, and live at peace. However, it was a huge deal. It opened up the leader of Israel to the pagan influences of other gods.

> *King Solomon, however, loved many foreign women besides Pharaoh's daughter—Moabites, Ammonites, Edomites, Sidonians and Hittites. They were from nations about which the LORD had told the Israelites, "You must not intermarry with them, because they will surely turn your hearts after their gods." Nevertheless, Solomon held fast to them in love.*

Solomon made lots of these marriage treaties. He knew it was disobedience against God, but the one marriage didn't seem to really affect his reign too much. If it worked once, why not do it again? The more Solomon compromised with these wives, the easier it got. It eventually got out of control.

> *He had seven hundred wives of royal birth and three hundred concubines, and his wives led him astray. As Solomon grew old, his wives turned his heart after other gods, and his heart was not fully devoted to the LORD his God, as the heart of David his father had been. He followed Ashtoreth the goddess of the Sidonians, and Molek the detestable god of the Ammonites. So Solomon did evil in the eyes of the LORD; he did not follow the LORD completely, as David his father had done.*

WHAT!! Seven hundred wives!! Three hundred mistresses?? Are you kidding me? Let's not even get into discussing how his compromise landed him seven hundred mothers-in-law to deal with! Not to men-tion three hundred other mothers asking him when he was going to commit to *their* daughters!

Solomon's little acts of compromise eventually ballooned out of control, causing him to stop following God wholeheartedly. He didn't serve him in the way God had commanded. He began to worship other gods as well. However, his compromise still didn't end here.

> *On a hill east of Jerusalem, Solomon built a high place for Chemosh the detestable god of Moab, and for Molek the detestable god of the Ammonites. He did the same for all his foreign wives, who burned incense and offered sacrifices to their gods.*

Solomon, the man who had built God's holy temple, had compromised himself so much that he began building temples for his wives' gods. He had obtained the ultimate blessing of God on his life after he built the holy temple, but his new building projects would take these blessings away.

> *The LORD became angry with Solomon because his heart had turned away from the LORD, the God of Israel, who had appeared to him twice. Although he had forbidden Solomon to follow other gods, Solomon did not keep the LORD's command. So the LORD said to Solomon, "Since this is your attitude and you have not kept my covenant and my decrees, which I commanded you, I will most certainly tear the kingdom away from you and give it to one of your subordinates."*

Solomon had begun his reign walking in complete obedience to God. He enjoyed wealth, peace, and the blessing of God. He had the world at his feet! However, compromising what he knew was right ended up costing him everything God had given him.

Ironically, it came directly from the area he had sought to avoid through his compromise. Solomon used intermarriage with the pagan leaders' daughters to try and achieve peace. It ended up being the one thing God used to punish him!

The Bible tells us that God raised up enemies to torment Solomon for the rest of his days as king.

Bye-bye, peace! Hello, results of compromise! He compromised to receive peace, but all he ended up with was war, sorrow, and loss of God's blessing.

Solomon's life demonstrates a lesson we all need to learn: compromising may gain us what we want in the short term, but in the long term it leads us down a path of loss, sin, heartbreak, and eventually separation from God.

Each time we compromise just a little, it makes it easier to do it again. Solomon started out as a man wholly devoted to God. However, he compromised his beliefs slightly to get what he wanted.

He didn't stop serving God, but he wasn't as vigorous as he had been.

Slowly, he let other things creep in until he had gone so far as serving other gods and building them temples.

Guys, compromise is devastating to our walk with God. The main reason for this is because it goes side by side with our relationship with God. We don't see the damage because we are still serving God. The compromise lulls us into complacency. Slowly, we lose our zeal and desire to serve God completely. It happens so gradually that we don't see how it is destroying us until it is too late.

Compromise is an issue that we all face. The Christian community is faced with more areas to compromise than ever before. We are tempted to compromise politically, morally, financially, and spiritually. People use the words of Paul that say they have freedom in Christ to do whatever they want. They totally ignore Paul's command not to use his words as an excuse to sin.

Too many believers are getting as close to the line as they can. However, this is dangerous. Each time we compromise, the line moves a little bit. Eventually, we are so far over the line that we can't even see it anymore. Our relationship with God gets lost and we don't even realize it.

I know that there was a time in my life when compromise damaged my spiritual life. I grew up with a strong, godly mother who instilled godly convictions and beliefs into my life. She taught me the importance of prayer, Bible reading, and standing for what I believe in. While there were times I struggled with rebellion and disobedience, for the most part I stood for what I believed.

When I graduated from high school, I enrolled in Bible college. Because of the abuse in my past as well as the many physical problems I faced throughout my life, I struggled with feeling like "a real man." I didn't feel I was as good as the other guys. In my own eyes, I didn't measure up to them. I constantly felt the need to prove my manhood. In order to fit in, I began setting aside my convictions and compromising to be one of the guys.

It started with little things like the style of clothes I wore. I started wearing more popular but less flattering styles. I changed my hairstyle to be like everyone else. Then I changed the style of music I would listen to. I stopped listening to groups I loved and started listening to groups I didn't really enjoy, just to fit in.

Next came TV viewing. I watched old, classic shows. The other guys preferred newer, more action-packed shows or reality TV. I wasn't comfortable with some of the content of these shows, but to fit in, I watched them.

I changed my eating habits, sleeping patterns, and study habits in order to be one of the guys. Eventually, video games and naps become more important to me than time spent in the Bible. I justified my compromise by telling myself I was still okay with God. I used the Bible for classes, why did I have to read it in devotions?

I stopped going to church. I justified this by telling myself that I went to required chapel services every day. God wouldn't mind if I skipped church and caught up on much-needed sleep before watching football with the guys. Slowly, my compromises chipped away at who I was as a person and as a Christian until they made me into a person I neither knew nor liked.

My more liberal TV viewing whet an appetite in me, and I started watching more sensual movies alone. I told myself it was no big deal because I wasn't watching porn. However, the fire was fueled, and I eventually started watching online porn. Before I knew it, I was trapped. All because of little compromises I made in the beginning.

I am thankful God put an end to my compromising. He pointed it out and made me face it and deal with it. I had to repent of all the ways I had compromised. I had to face how it started and the issues that caused me to begin changing who I was. I began to realize how slowly it occurred. I repented, took back any ground I had given to the enemy through my compromising, and started again with God.

> **Guys, this is the good news about compromise: at any time we can stop doing it. We can face it, turn around, and begin to live wholeheartedly before God.**

Guys, this is the good news about compromise: at any time we can stop doing it. We can face it, turn around, and begin to live wholeheartedly before God. How do I know this? Solomon tells us so.

At the end of Solomon's life, he realized how much compromise had cost him. In the book of Ecclesiastes, he discusses all the ways he had compromised his relationship with God. After each example, he tells us that it was all useless. It had come at too high of a price. He concludes the book by telling us what he learned from his years of compromise.

Now all has been heard; here is the conclusion of the matter: Fear God and keep his commandments, for this is the duty of all mankind. For God will bring every deed into judgment, including every hidden thing, whether it is good or evil.

Solomon's life of compromise had taught him that it wasn't worth it. The only thing that will bring about a good result to our lives is to fear God, follow him, and obey his commands. This, not compromise, is the only way to grow into a mature, godly man. It alone allows us to experience the promises of God in our lives.

Guys, we need to take this chapter very seriously. Why? Because compromise is deadly to us, and, because it is so subtle, we rarely can identify it in ourselves. Thankfully, we have the Holy Spirit whose job is to shine his light of truth and conviction on our lives to show us our areas of compromise.

As we wrap up this chapter, let's allow him to do his job.

Are there areas of compromise that have crept into your life?

What are some decisions or actions you have taken that you knew were wrong, but you did it anyway?

When did you make this decision? What were you doing? What was going on in your life at the time?

How have these compromises affected your life? Your relationship with God? What can you do to break free from these compromises?

These are all excellent questions to ask the Holy Spirit. The question is, are you man enough to let him show you the answers?

I urge you to take this chapter seriously. Learn from Solomon's example that the cost of compromise is too great. It is not worth it.

The truth is that the slope of compromise has kept many who were destined for greatness in God's kingdom from ever reaching their potential. Men who could have been in God's Hall of Fame were sidelined as they fumbled not just once but over and over again until they were completely out of the game. The compromise that initially seemed like no big deal devoured their whole lives, ultimately eliminating them from the game and relegating them to the position of losers and spectators.

But it doesn't have to be this way.

Today, each of us can choose to avoid compromise. Even if you find yourself trapped in this cycle, you can choose to end the cycle today and get back into shape spiritually.

How do we do it? What is the game plan to overcome compromise?

We must daily examine ourselves to make sure compromise hasn't reared its ugly head in our lives.

We must face any areas head on, repent of them, and make changes to follow God wholeheartedly.

From this point on we must refuse to lose by refusing to compromise but clinging to the standards and principles taught in God's Word.

By doing this, we can become all that God wants us to be. We must begin today.

Dear heavenly Father, Please forgive me for any time I have allowed compromise and sin to interfere with my relationship with you. Please point out any and all areas of compromise. Show me when they started and what caused them so that I can face them, deal with them, and destroy them completely. I no longer want any areas of compromise to affect my relationship with you. In Jesus' name, amen.

TRAINING DRILL

At the end of this chapter we listed some questions to ask yourself. Take time to get alone with the Holy Spirit and a notepad. Allow him to show you the truthful answer to the questions. Write down areas where you have compromised, repent of them, and commit to change.

TWO-A-DAYS

Share the list you made in the homework section with a trusted friend or mentor and ask him to hold you accountable. Also, ask him if he sees areas of compromise in you that you missed.

TEAM MEETING

1. Define *compromise.*

2. In this chapter we said, "Each time we compromise just a little, it makes it easier to do it again." What does this mean to you?

3. Are there areas of compromise that have crept into your life?

4. How has compromise affected the church community?

5. What can we as a group do to keep compromise from destroying our men's group and our church community?

6. How do we defeat compromise?

7. What stands out to you the most about Solomon's story? What did you learn from studying his game footage to help you avoid the trap he fell into in his life?

8. How can we as a group help you?

CHAPTER 9

SHINING A LIGHT ON THE DARK CORNERS

It's the end of the day and a man is closing up the shop for the night. He is in a hurry to get to the softball league game he has that evening. He just has one job to do. The boss trusted him to close down the cash register, fill out the financial report, and deposit the money in the bank. As he counts the money and gets it ready, he slips a ten dollar bill in his pocket. He has been doing it for the past few months, and has accumulated a nice little nest egg. He sees nothing wrong with it, it is only ten dollars; no one misses it, it is just his little secret.

Meanwhile, across the country, a man is on a business trip. He is a little bummed that he is going to miss playing in his softball league this week, but his job has to take precedence. At the meeting, he strikes up a conversation with another employee of the company named Tiffany. Tiffany is young and attractive, and he enjoys talking with her. She enjoyed it too, because she asks him if he wants to grab a bite to eat after the meeting. He unconsciously slips his hand with his wedding ring in his pocket as he thinks about the offer. He knows he shouldn't do it, but he is far from home and no one will ever know. It will just be their secret.

Later that night, another guy is slipping into his local convenience store wearing a hat and sunglasses. He is sweaty and dirty after playing catcher in a league game. He self-consciously looks around as he walks to the cooler, reaches in, and grabs a six-pack. He quickly pays and bolts for his car, hoping no one notices him buying alcohol. He feels a twinge of guilt that he is drinking again, but he quickly pushes it aside. After all, it is his secret, who would know?

Later that night, a man is looking at his wife sound asleep next to him, but he is restless and unable to doze off. He is still pumped up from hitting the game-winning home run in his softball game, catapulting his team into the playoffs. He decides to get back up and work on his presentation for the big business meeting.

As he searches the net for a good graphic for his presentation, a pop-up flies on his screen. He sees an ad with a scantily clad woman on it. He know he vowed last time he looked that it would be his last time, but everything inside of him says, "Look at it, it will relax you enough to sleep." Two clicks later, he's back in the stuff that secretly has bound him for years. But who is going to know? It is just his little secret.

A few days later, four guys are sitting in a local diner to have a bite together before heading over to play in their church softball league. These four guys had committed to showing up early each week to spend time together before the game. It was how they did their weekly accountability group as they lived life together. As they sit and talk, Bill mentions how great work has been going lately. He tells how his boss has him closing up every night and making the deposits. His friend says "See, that's the power of God in you that makes him able to trust you with his money. Aren't you ever tempted to help yourself to some of it?"

Bill instantly panics. He knows he was the man lifting ten dollars a month from his boss. He can't let this secret out! So he quickly changes the subject by redirecting the conversation to Dave.

"Hey Dave, you been sleeping okay lately? I noticed Facebook had you logged in at 1 a.m. the other night."

Dave begins to panic. How could he be so stupid as to not log out of Facebook? What if Bill figures out what he *really* was doing when he was suppose to be working on his presentation after not being able to sleep? He began to make some kind of excuse, but he is saved by Tom's annoying ringtone.

"Man, Tom, shut that stupid song off, it is so annoying!" he jokes. He reaches over and grabs Tom's cell phone before he can grab it.

"Hey Tom, who is Tiffany? She is texting you to call her when you have some free time."

Tom's heart drops! How does he explain Tiffany? He told her not to call him on his phone. Now Dave saw her text!

Tom quickly makes up a lie and says, "Oh, Tiffany is an intern at the office. She probably just can't find a file. I'll call her when we're done."

Tom looks around at the guys. He thinks they bought his story, but to make sure, he quickly turns the attention to Jason. "Jason, how long has it been now since you got saved? It's got to be what, two years? I'll never forget how God saved you and delivered you from drinking. Are you ever tempted to drink again?"

Jason calmly says, "Nah, I am done with alcohol. But you know what, I had better head to the field. It takes forever to get the catcher's gear on, and it's almost time for the game."

But inside he is panicking. He had just finished the last of the six-pack he bought at the convenience store after the last game. Why did Tom have to ask him about it?

The four men quickly finished up their meeting, deciding they had better get to the field and get warmed up for the game. They are all anxious to get out of there before any more pointed questions are asked. After all, they need to make sure their secret sin stays just that—a secret. They get to the game and start throwing the ball around, all feeling guilty over their secret sin, but none willing to admit it.

While using extreme, stereotypical examples, this is a story that is repeated over and over in our world today. Christian men across America have issues of secret sin in their lives that they work diligently to keep concealed. They fear anyone finding out because it would destroy their reputations as men of God. So they continue in their secret sin, secretly wishing they could be free of it, but not taking steps to overcome.

Guys, this should not be so! Secret sin is a dangerous thing to be playing around with, especially when the God of the universe stands waiting with his gift of freedom.

Too many men are rejecting this gift and exchanging it for the secret sin they think they have hidden away so well. However, this is a dangerous game, and it is not the game we are called to be a part of in life.

How do I know this? There is a man in the Bible who shows us the tremendous cost of exchanging God's blessings for our hidden sins. His name is Achan.

Achan's story is found in my favorite book of the Old Testament, Joshua. The people of Israel are moving toward the land that was promised to them by God, and he is miraculously helping them defeat enemy after enemy that is standing between them and God's promises.

We read about Achan immediately after an amazing victory for the children of Israel as God single-handedly destroyed the walls of Jericho. Once the wall was gone, Joshua and his men were able to rout the city. However, before they entered the city, they learned exactly what it was God wanted them to do. Let's look at Joshua 6 (NKJV).

And you, by all means abstain from the accursed things, lest you become accursed when you take of the accursed things, and make the camp of Israel a curse, and trouble it. But all the silver and gold, and vessels of bronze and iron, are consecrated to the LORD; they shall come into the treasury of the LORD."

God made it perfectly clear to them that they were not to loot the city of Jericho for personal gain. They were to kill all the people in the city except Rahab and her family. They were also supposed to burn everything in the city, except the silver, gold, and bronze which were supposed to go to the Lord's treasury. Sounds easy enough, right? As we continue on, we see it is harder than we think.

But the children of Israel committed a trespass regarding the accursed things, for Achan the son of Carmi, the son of Zabdi, the son of Zerah, of the tribe of Judah, took of the accursed things; so the anger of the LORD burned against the children of Israel

One of Joshua's men, Achan, disobeyed the orders of God. He committed treason by disobeying his CO's commands. He took some of the plunder and hid it under his tent. However, his actions were unknown to Joshua. All Joshua knew was that they had just won an amazing victory. Now was the time to strike again.

Now Joshua sent men from Jericho to Ai, which is beside Beth Aven, on the east side of Bethel, and spoke to them, saying, "Go up and spy out the country." So the men went up and spied out Ai.

Joshua set his sights on the city of Ai. After the stunning victory at Jericho, he was sure the people could defeat this tiny city. The report from his spies only bolstered that opinion.

And they returned to Joshua and said to him, "Do not let all the people go up, but let about two or three thousand men go up and attack Ai. Do not weary all the people there, for the people of Ai are few." So about three thousand men went up there from the people, but they fled before the men of Ai. And the men of Ai struck down about thirty-six men, for they chased them from before the gate as far as Shebarim, and struck them down on the descent; therefore the hearts of the people melted and became like water.

What?! This wasn't supposed to happen. They lost the battle! What was going on? What happened to God and his power? These are the questions we naturally would ask, and they are exactly what we hear from Joshua.

Then Joshua tore his clothes, and fell to the earth on his face before the ark of the LORD until evening, he and the elders of Israel; and they put dust on their heads. And Joshua said, "Alas, Lord GOD, why have You brought this people over the Jordan at all—to deliver us into the hand of the Amorites, to destroy us? Oh, that we had been content, and dwelt on the other side of the Jordan! O Lord, what shall I say when Israel turns its back before its enemies? For the Canaanites and all the inhabitants of the land will hear it, and surround us, and cut off our name from the earth. Then what will You do for Your great name?"

Joshua did what many of us would do. He blamed God.

He told God that God had failed his people. He felt God had set them up only to have them be defeated by their enemies. He basically told God that he had made himself look bad.

However, Joshua didn't know the whole story, but God did. He quickly put Joshua in his place!

So the LORD said to Joshua: "Get up! Why do you lie thus on your face? Israel has sinned, and they have also transgressed My covenant which I commanded them. For they have even taken some of the accursed things, and have both stolen and deceived; and they have also put it among their own stuff. Therefore the children of

Israel could not stand before their enemies, but turned their backs before their enemies, because they have become doomed to destruction. Neither will I be with you anymore, unless you destroy the accursed from among you."

God basically said to Joshua, "Listen Sparky, this is not my fault. Your people disobeyed me. They committed treason against me. I can't fight for you when you disobey me. Until you make things right, your enemies will defeat you."

We can now see the cost of secret sin. Achan, one of God's children, took something he was forbidden to take, and hid it. He had this secret stash hidden away, and only he knew about it. At least that's what he thought! God knew, and God refused to condone hidden sin among his people.

Guys, our secret sin is serious stuff. It destroys everything. It not only causes separation between us and God, but it affects others around us. Achan is the perfect demonstration of this truth! Let's continue on with the passage to see what I mean.

> *"Get up, sanctify the people, and say, 'Sanctify yourselves for tomorrow, because thus says the LORD God of Israel: "There is an accursed thing in your midst, O Israel; you cannot stand before your enemies until you take away the accursed thing from among you."'"*

God commanded Joshua to remove the sin from the camp. If

God can't bless us or give us spiritual victories when we are hiding secret sin. Until we consecrate ourselves and remove the sin, we won't experience the blessing of God in our lives or defeat our spiritual enemies.

the secret sin was not exposed and dealt with, then Israel would never defeat their enemies.

The same is true for us. God can't bless us or give us spiritual victories when we are hiding secret sin. Until we consecrate ourselves and remove the sin, we won't experience the blessing of God in our lives or defeat our spiritual enemies.

When we try and hold on to our pet sins and keep them hidden and secret, we will not only destroy ourselves, but it will affect those around us. It certainly affected those around Achan.

We already read that thirty-six men lost their lives and the entire nation's military reputation was ruined. However, the effects didn't end there.

"In the morning therefore you shall be brought according to your tribes. And it shall be that the tribe which the LORD takes shall come according to families; and the family which the LORD takes shall come by households; and the household which the LORD takes shall come man by man. Then it shall be that he who is taken with the accursed thing shall be burned with fire, he and all that he has, because he has transgressed the covenant of the LORD, and because he has done a disgraceful thing in Israel."

So Joshua rose early in the morning and brought Israel by their tribes, and the tribe of Judah was taken. He brought the clan of Judah, and he took the family of the Zarhites; and he brought the family of the Zarhites man by man, and Zabdi was taken. Then he brought his household man by man, and Achan the son of Carmi, the son of Zabdi, the son of Zerah, of the tribe of Judah, was taken.

Achan's sin caused his entire tribe to suffer. They were all placed under suspicion because of his act of deliberate sin.

Now Joshua said to Achan, "My son, I beg you, give glory to the Lord God of Israel, and make confession to Him, and tell me now what you have done; do not hide it from me."

And Achan answered Joshua and said, "Indeed I have sinned against the Lord God of Israel, and this is what I have done: When I saw among the spoils a beautiful Babylonian garment, two hundred shekels of silver, and a wedge of gold weighing fifty shekels, I coveted them and took them. And there they are, hidden in the earth in the midst of my tent, with the silver under it."

Achan's hidden secret was exposed by God. He tells Joshua the great sin he had committed. However, it was not a repentant confession. Achan doesn't show the sorrow or remorse that accompanies true repentance.

He never willing stepped forward and confessed. He was simply caught. He had no choice but to state the facts of what he had done.

Deliberately choosing to hide sins from God causes people to harden their hearts. The more they do it, the easier it gets until they feel no remorse and see no shame in what they have done.

Achan seems to have reached this point. He showed no concern for the thirty-six lives he had caused to die. He shows no regret for what he put his family through. He doesn't care that he offended God, causing God to stop fighting for Israel. He just coldly states the facts of his sin.

Joshua is now furious. He sent men to examine the facts to see if Achan was telling the truth. Once the story is confirmed, Joshua took Achan outside the camp and pronounces his judgment.

Then Joshua, and all Israel with him, took Achan the son of Zerah, the silver, the garment, the wedge of gold, his sons, his daughters, his oxen, his donkeys, his sheep, his tent, and all that he had, and they brought them to the Valley of Achor. And Joshua said, "Why have you troubled us? The Lord will trouble you this day." So all Israel stoned him with stones; and they burned them with fire after they had stoned them with stones. Then they raised over him a great heap of stones, still there to this day. So the LORD turned from the fierceness of His anger. Therefore the name of that place has been called the Valley of Achor to this day.

Achan, along with his family, was put to death and all his possessions were burned. What had begun as a week of joy and victory for Israel had turned into one of defeat, sorrow, and judgment. Guys, hidden, secret sin certainly has its price.

This story cannot be taken too lightly or passed over quickly. We must take it very seriously.

Achan was a man just like us.

He was a follower of God.

He experienced God's power.

He had promises on his life.

However, because he willfully chose to sin against God and then tried to hide his sin, he lost it all.

Achan never defeated his enemies.

He never built his home in the Promised Land.

He never grew old with his family.

He lost any relationship with God.

He lost all of his family and possessions.

He died as a rebellious traitor.

While he had the opportunity to earn a place in the Hall of Fame as one of Israel's warriors, he is forever known as a wicked man responsible for Israel's loss on the battlefield. All of this happened because he chose to keep sin hidden in his life. We need to be careful we don't do the same thing.

Secret sins have devastating consequences. We see in the passage that Achan's family was put to death because of his actions. Guys, our secret sins have can have a far-reaching effects.

Let's use the examples we started this chapter with to show what I mean. Each man had an area of hidden sin. If each area of sin were exposed, it would definitely destroy any witness these men think they have for God. But it goes even further.

Bill was secretly stealing money. When, not if, he gets caught, his family will suffer tremendously. His wife and children will be devastated to learn that the man of God they lived with was really a liar and a thief. Bill will face a trial and possibly jail, separating him from his family. His kids will bear the shame of having a father in prison.

Dave was up late viewing porn. When, not if, his secret sin is exposed, his marriage will be devastated. His wife will feel dirty. She will lose all faith and trust in him. The men in his small group will feel betrayed because he refused to ask them for help.

Tom is fooling around with Tiffany from work. Think that's going to end well? When, not if, this secret is exposed, his family will be devastated by his affair. Statistics show his wife will probably leave him. He will go from being an active dad to having periodic visitation with his children. Friends will take sides, some will stay friends with him, others will abandon him and side with his wife. His testimony will be ruined, and his band of brothers will be left stunned at his lies to them.

Jason is slipping back into his alcoholism. When, not if, his lack of sobriety is exposed, everyone around him will lose trust in him. His friends, family, and band of brothers will be heartbroken that he not only fell back into the bondage of the bottle, but that he lied to them about it.

What if he decides to hop into his car while drunk? He could lose his license, and his job. He could get caught and face huge fines or jail time. He could hurt others on the road. That could have far-reaching effects on countless lives! The testimony of his amazing conversion and deliverance from alcoholism will be destroyed.

Guys, secret sins devastate. Notice in each case I said, "when, not if." Your secret sin *will* come to light. It will be less devastating to humbly confess and admit your need for help than it will be to have it exposed by someone else.

Why?

Because while it may be a secret to everyone else, God knows all about it. He hates seeing his children trapped in secret sin, and he will expose you.

Secret sins are one of the biggest ways Satan traps men. He makes them think they can continue to do what they do in secret. After all, it isn't hurting anyone, no one else knows. He encourages men to keep their sin hidden. However, he doesn't tell men the whole story.

> **Notice in each case I said, "when, not if." Your secret sin will come to light. Why? Because while it may be a secret to everyone else, God knows all about it. He hates seeing his children trapped in secret sin, and he will expose you.**

The whole story is that Satan wants you to stay bound in secret sins so one day he can expose you! He wants to expose what it is you are doing in secret so he can destroy you, your life, your relationship with God, and your relationship with others. He wants to shout to the world what you do in secret to humiliate you.

Satan is not the only person who wants to reveal your secret sins. God's goal is to shout your secret sins from the rooftop. How do I know this? Because the Bible says so!

- *Luke 12:2–3 There is nothing concealed that will not be disclosed, or hidden that will not be made known. What you have said in the dark will be heard in the daylight, and what you have whispered in the ear in the inner rooms will be proclaimed from the roofs.*

- *Luke 8:17* (ESV) *For nothing is hidden that will not be made manifest, nor is anything secret that will not be known and come to light.*

- *Hebrews 4:13* (ESV) *And no creature is hidden from his sight, but all are naked and exposed to the eyes of him to whom we must give account.*

- *Ecclesiastes 12:14* *For God will bring every deed into judgment, including every hidden thing, whether it is good or evil.*

- *Psalm 44:21* (ESV) *Would not God discover this? For he knows the secrets of the heart.*

- *Romans 2:16* (ESV) *On that day when, according to my gospel, God judges the secrets of men by Christ Jesus.*

- *Luke 12:3* (ESV) *Therefore whatever you have said in the dark shall be heard in the light, and what you have whispered in private rooms shall be proclaimed on the housetops.*

- *Psalms 90:8* (ESV) *You have set our iniquities before you, our secret sins in the light of your presence.*

- *Jeremiah 23:23–24* *"Am I only a God nearby," declares the* LORD, *"And not a God far away? Who can hide in secret places so that I cannot see them?" declares the* LORD.

These verses show us that nothing is hidden from God. We may be able to hide our secret sins from others, but God sees it all! Not only does he see it all, but these verses show us that he is going to expose our secret sin.

God wants to expose you and your secret sin because he loves you and wants to set you free. He wants it to come to light to save you. Satan wants to do it to destroy you. If two such powerful forces are bound and determined to expose your secret sin, then how do we think we can ever keep it hidden?

It is time for men of God to stand up and say enough is enough! We refuse to lose because of hidden sins! It is time we overcome our secret sins! I firmly believe it is time for men of God to shine the light of truth on our lives and to gain freedom from our secret sins. It is time we stand up and say, "I am trapped in the sin of _____ and I want to be free, and I don't care who knows it!"

How do we do it?

We do it by becoming tattletales. Remember when we were kids, there was always one kid who always told all the secrets or turned you in if he knew you did something wrong? You know, the kid that got beat up a lot. This kid was usually labeled a tattletale. Well, it is time we become spiritual tattletales on ourselves.

> It is time for men of God to stand up and say enough is enough! It is time to shine the light of truth on our lives and to gain freedom from our secret sins. It is time we stand up and say, "I am trapped in sin, I want to be free, and I don't care who knows it!"

What should have happened at the pre-game accountability meeting we described above was four brothers in Christ should have been honest and confessed their sins to each other. They should have tattled on themselves by confessing their secret sin.

Secrets lose their power when the light of truth and honesty are shown on them. So the first step to revealing our secret sin is to out ourselves and confess the secret.

The next step is to repent.

Take David as an example. In the Bible, King David was a man with everything. He had God's blessing on his life. He had loyal subjects. He had wives, children, wealth, all a man could ask for. But one night, while taking a stroll on the palace roof, he saw a beautiful woman taking a bath. He looked, he lusted, and then he acted on his lust.

He had the woman brought to him and had sex with her, knowing she was a married woman; actually, she was the wife of one of his oldest warriors and friends who stood by him during the hardest time of his life. He betrayed one of his mighty men by sleeping with his wife. However, no one knew about it. Until she became pregnant!

David's secret sin was about to become public, so he took action to keep it hidden. He devised a plan to have his faithful warrior, who had been with him since before he was king, come home from battle and sleep with his wife, causing everyone to think her pregnancy was from her husband. However, her husband was so loyal to David that he refused to go to his wife when he should have been fighting for David. So David took the ultimate step to keep his sin hidden. He had his mighty man killed! He murdered a trusted ally, all to keep his sin a secret.

However, as we mentioned, God loved David too much to allow him to be trapped in hidden sin, so he exposed David's secret sin. He was exposed to everyone. However, unlike Achan who was unrepentant and lost it all, David fell to his knees and repented. His repentance is found in Psalms 51.

Have mercy on me, O God, according to your unfailing love; according to your great compassion blot out my transgressions. Wash away all my iniquity and cleanse me from my sin.

For I know my transgressions, and my sin is always before me. Against you, you only, have I sinned and done what is evil in your sight; so you are right in your verdict and justified when you judge. ...Create in me a pure heart, O God, and renew a steadfast spirit within me. Do not cast me from your presence or take your Holy Spirit from me. Restore to me the joy of your salvation and grant me a willing spirit, to sustain me.

Unlike Achan, David responded properly when his secret sins were exposed. He repented. He made things right with God. Using our book's sports analogy, when he coughed up the ball, he quickly jumped on top of it, recovering so he could continue toward the end zone.

I encourage you, if you have hidden sin in your life, follow David's example, not Achan's. You also need to confess the sin to God and ask for forgiveness.

Why do you need to confess the sin if God already knows about it?

Because it kills our flesh to expose ourselves to God. It breaks the power the secret has over us. When we expose the secret sin, it frees us. So we have to confess to God and to others and ask forgiveness and deliverance from our secret sin.

Next, you have to go Rambo on your secret sin!

You have to go to extremes with your sin.

You need to make restitution if your secret sin requires it (i.e., financial sins, etc.).

You have to open yourself up to accountability until it hurts.

You need fellow brothers in Christ who will be relentless in holding you accountable, and you need to be honest with them about everything.

Finally, you have to commit yourself to living in honesty and integrity. All the confessing, repenting, and accountability in the world are useless if you are not committed to being free.

That is why secret sin is so crippling; it is really up to you if you overcome or not. But if you will set your heart to live free of your secret sin, if you surrender daily to the Holy Spirit's control, and if you will submit to the authority and accountability of others, you can be free of secret sin. If you don't do this, your secret sin will destroy you.

That is as plain as I can say it. The decision is yours today. Will you conquer your secret sin? I hope your answer is a resounding YES!

Dear heavenly Father, I come to you today to confess my secret sin of _____. I have been hiding this sin from you and everyone around me. Forgive me for thinking I could get away with this sin because no one knew about it. Forgive me for holding on to it and allowing it a place in my life.

Father, I ask you to give me victory over this sin. Give me the courage to shine the light of truth onto this area of sin that I have kept hidden in the dark places. Help me open myself up to accountability to I can conquer this area of sin.

Thank you Father for your forgiveness and grace. Help me as I go forward, leaving my hidden sins behind me. In Jesus' name, amen.

TRAINING DRILL

The only way to remove hidden sin is to expose it. After you confess your sin to God, find a **mature, trustworthy** believer and confess your sin to him. Ask him to help you overcome.

TWO-A-DAYS

Secret sin is so dangerous because only you and God know about it. Blow this to smithereens by opening yourself to accountability. Meet weekly with an accountability partner and allow him to ask you anything he wants about any area of your life and answer him honestly.

TEAM MEETING

1. What is the danger of hidden sins?

2. Why does Satan want to expose secret sins?

3. Why does God want to expose secret sins?

4. How can secret sins affect our families?

5. How can secret sins affect our small group?

6. How can secret sins affect our church?

7. What place does accountability have in defeating secret sins?

8. Knowing that what happens in the group stays in the group, does anyone have anything they need to confess after reading this chapter?

CHAPTER 10

TRUTH IN BLACK & WHITE, AND ALL COLORS IN BETWEEN

Did you ever have a conversation with a fellow believer, and, as they talked, your jaw dropped open in stunned disbelief at the thing they just said? I remember one such time in my life.

A man I had known most of my life came to visit us. Earlier in his life, this man had helped found a church, was a church leader for many years, and was known by everyone as a Christian. However, as he stood there talking to my father, this man started saying some of the most hateful things I had ever heard. He referred to other ethnicities by cruel and vulgar names. He criticized them, their work habits, and their lifestyles, all based on the color of their skin. I was stunned!

I wasn't used to this kind of talk. I was raised to respect everyone despite ethnicity or skin color. I honestly never heard such things spoken by a fellow Christian. That night, I lost any respect I ever had for this man. I often think about that night and wonder why a Christian would allow himself to be filled with such disgusting hate.

Unfortunately, this man is not alone in his attitudes and behavior. There are many people who follow God, serve in their churches, and are well-respected in their communities who struggle with prejudice in their lives.

I know another Christian man who was a leader in his church, but thought it was funny to tell semi-racist jokes. At first, I thought it was just inappropriate humor and not a prejudiced attitude. Then I heard this man's child make a blatantly racist comment. Children don't think of these things themselves, they hear it at home, so apparently this man's issues ran deeper than just joking around.

You may be reading this and be tempted to skip to the next chapter. Maybe you're thinking, "Jamie, I am not prejudiced. I have lots of friends of other races."

I encourage you to continue reading. Prejudice comes in more ways than just the color of people's skins. Prejudice comes in many forms, whether it be age, class, career, or even gender. Guys, there can be no place for prejudice in a Christian's heart and life. It is time we all shine light on the dark area of prejudice in our lives and take steps to destroy any prejudice we find.

In this chapter, we are going to examine the life of a man who could have given the title of "The World's Greatest Evangelist." He preached to and converted an entire nation's capital city. However, because of his prejudice, he is never remembered for his amazing evangelistic success. As we study this man, we will see how costly prejudice is to our pursuit of becoming like Jesus. Let's get started as we study the life and ministry of Jonah.

A PREJUDICED PROPHET

Nearly everyone is familiar with the story of Jonah. Many sermons have been preached on the way Jonah's disobedience caused him to become whale bait. All the analogies have been made and all the puke jokes have been told. However, in this chapter, I want us to examine the reason behind Jonah's fleeing from God. The reason Jonah became the sushi of the day can be summed up in one sentence: Jonah was a bigot.

To understand why I say this, we need to examine Jonah's actions.

The word of the LORD came to Jonah son of Amittai: "Go to the great city of Nineveh and preach against it, because its wickedness has come up before me."

Jonah was given the great privilege of speaking the Word of God to the city of Nineveh. Nineveh was the extremely rich and influential capital of the nation of Assyria.

Assyria was also one of Israel's biggest enemies. They beat, abused, and oppressed them. A good Jew would pray for the blessing of God on the nation of Israel and his judgment on Assyria. Jonah was not about to go preach to those people! He didn't want them saved. He wanted them dead! As a result, Jonah ran away from God and ended up spending three days in the whale.

Inside of the whale, Jonah made peace with God. It's funny how many people surrender their will to God and do what he wants when they are stuck in horrible circumstances. Once Jonah surrenders to God, God causes the whale to puke Jonah out. He must have landed close to the shores of Nineveh, for we read he immediately enters the city.

Jonah obeyed the word of the LORD and went to Nineveh. Now Nineveh was a very large city; it took three days to go through it. Jonah began by going a day's journey into the city, proclaiming, "Forty more days and Nineveh will be overthrown." The Ninevites believed God. A fast was proclaimed, and all of them, from the greatest to the least, put on sackcloth.

When Jonah's warning reached the king of Nineveh, he rose from his throne, took off his royal robes, covered himself with sackcloth and sat down in the dust. ...When God saw what they did and how they turned from their evil ways, he relented and did not bring on them the destruction he had threatened.

Jonah led one of the greatest revival services in history. It reached from the poorest beggars to the greatest politicians. The entire city repented and turned to God. You would expect Jonah to be thrilled at the success of his efforts. However, he wasn't. His bigotry and hatred for the people of Nineveh ran too deep. Instead of praising God for their salvation, Jonah ran to the desert for a good pout.

But to Jonah this seemed very wrong, and he became angry. He prayed to the LORD, "Isn't this what I said, LORD, when I was still at home? That is what I tried to forestall by fleeing to Tarshish. I knew that you are a gracious and compassionate God, slow to anger and abounding in love, a God who relents from sending calamity. Now, LORD, take away my life, for it is better for me to die than to live."

"EVERY PARTY HAS A POOPER AND THAT'S WHY WE INVITED YOU!"

Jonah is actually angry about the way his revival stories turned out! Jonah is throwing himself one of the biggest pity parties ever recorded in the annals of history. He is mad at God for saving, not destroying, his enemies.

God in no way appreciated the prejudice and hatred in Jonah's heart. He speaks directly to Jonah.

But the LORD replied, "Is it right for you to be angry?"

God asks Jonah the obvious question. Instead of answering God, Jonah did what he does best. He ran away. However, this time he had an evil motive. He wanted to wait it out and see if the people are judged or not.

Jonah had gone out and sat down at a place east of the city. There he made himself a shelter, sat in its shade and waited to see what would happen to the city. Then the LORD God provided a leafy plant and made it grow up over Jonah to give shade for his head to ease his discomfort, and Jonah was very happy about the plant.

It seems odd that God appears to reward Jonah's prejudice and spoiled behavior. However, as we continue on, we see that it is no reward. God is setting Jonah up. He needs to let Jonah see the extent of hateful prejudice inside of his heart.

But at dawn the next day God provided a worm, which chewed the plant so that it withered. When the sun rose, God provided a scorching east wind, and the sun blazed on Jonah's head so that he grew faint. He wanted to die, and said, "It would be better for me to die than to live."

Can you say *drama queen?* What a stupid thing to say! Jonah is angry that God killed his plant instead of his enemies. Jonah feels that he, a Jew, deserved God's grace, not a dirty Assyrian! God now moves in for the kill. He makes a statement that is devastating to Jonah's prejudiced logic.

But God said to Jonah, "Is it right for you to be angry about the plant?"

"It is," he said. "And I'm so angry I wish I were dead."

But the LORD said, "You have been concerned about this plant, though you did not tend it or make it grow. It sprang up overnight and died overnight. And should I not have concern for the great city of Nineveh, in which there are more than a hundred and twenty thousand people who cannot tell their right hand from their left—and also many animals?"

Ouch! Jonah was put face to face with the prejudice in his heart. Of course, when God mentions people who don't know their right from their left, he is referring to infants and toddlers. God had to show Jonah how evil it was that he mourned the loss of his shade tree but would have loved to see the destruction of thousands of innocent Assyrian babies.

Jonah had no concern for their spiritual well being. Instead, he had anger and bigotry. This was not the heart of God and Jonah knew it. He had stated earlier that God was loving and compassionate. Jonah demonstrated none of these attributes. Let's return to the passage to see how things ended up for Jonah.

The word of the LORD that came to Micah of Moresheth... (Micah 1:1)

Prejudice is an ugly sin before God. It is really concealed hate.

"No wait, Jamie, Micah is the book of the Bible after Jonah!"

That's right. The story of Jonah ends with God's indictment of Jonah's prejudice. We have no idea what happens to Jonah. We have no clue if he changes his prejudiced heart. We don't read of any more revival meetings. For all we know, Jonah could have died in the wilderness, pouting next to a shriveled up plant. For all of history, Jonah is remembered not as a great evangelist, but as a prejudiced, angry man pouting in the wilderness.

Guys, prejudice is an ugly sin before God! Prejudice is really concealed hate. We all need to examine ourselves and remove even the slightest hint of prejudice. God commands us to show love to those around us. When we allow prejudice to have a place in our lives, we are giving ground to hatred. This is the exact opposite of God's heart. How do we know this? Because when Jesus walked the earth, he showed no prejudice at all to anyone.

Jesus loved everyone he encountered. He didn't condone their sin, but he loved and respected them. Whether it was tiny Zacheus, a Samaritan woman, a demon-possessed man chained to a headstone, a man with leprosy, a tax collector, or a rich young ruler, Jesus showed love to them all. He never turned anyone away because of how they looked. Social position meant nothing to Jesus. He looked at people's hearts and met whatever need they needed filled. He showed them love. We need to do the same.

We must show love to all people. We cannot be prejudiced. Some see prejudice as only against people of another color. However, it goes even deeper than that. Some are prejudiced against fat people. Others are prejudiced against sick people. Some are prejudiced against the rich while others despise the poor. Some Christians are prejudiced against the unsaved. Some show bigotry toward the elderly. Many men are prejudiced against women.

There is one *huge* area of prejudice in the Christian community that needs to end! Too many are prejudiced against young people. They don't want young people in their churches. They don't want their music in worship. They don't want their casual apparel in their services. This kind of thinking must stop!

But what about the souls of the young people? Will they ever step back inside a church again? Too often we allow our prejudice against "new" to cause us to lose sight of reaching younger people. Is it any wonder seven out of ten young people who grew up in the church leave for good?

No matter what the area of prejudice, it is sin and it must stop. We need to love one another. We need to respect each other. We must care for one another. We must never see appearance, status, or wealth. Instead we should see a soul in need of a Savior. All people have this same basic spiritual need no matter their age, race, sex, or social position.

Jonah didn't face the prejudice in his heart and it cost him everything. For all of history he is remembered as the prejudiced prophet. Watching his tape, it's easy to conclude that this is not the game plan that we want to follow.

But what do you do if you know you struggle with prejudice but you want to change?

For that answer, let's look at the life of another great evangelist: the apostle Nathanael.

Unlike most of the disciples, Nathanael was not called by Jesus. He was brought to Jesus by Philip. Philip and Nathanael were friends. When you read the account of Philip bringing Nathanael to Jesus, we learn a lot about Nathanael. John 1:43–48 says,

> *The next day Jesus decided to leave for Galilee. Finding Philip, he said to him, "Follow me."*
>
> *Philip, like Andrew and Peter, was from the town of Bethsaida. Philip found Nathanael and told him, "We have found the one Moses wrote about in the Law, and about whom the prophets also wrote—Jesus of Nazareth, the son of Joseph."*
>
> *"Nazareth! Can anything good come from there?" Nathanael asked.*
>
> *"Come and see," said Philip.*
>
> *When Jesus saw Nathanael approaching, he said of him, "Here truly is an Israelite in whom there is no deceit."*
>
> *"How do you know me?" Nathanael asked.*
>
> *Jesus answered, "I saw you while you were still under the fig tree before Philip called you."*

First, we see Nathaniel was devoted to studying God's Word. He was a man of prayer who studied God's Word for hours. He was a devout follower of God who longed for a deeper relationship with him.

Philip knew this and immediately went to get his friend so he, too, could follow Jesus. When Philip told Nathanael about Jesus, he basically says, "I found the Messiah we have been reading about during our men's Bible study."

The second thing we know about Nathanael is that he was a sincere man. When Philip brought Nathanael to Jesus, Jesus said that Nathanael was "a man without guile."

This means he had no hypocrisy; there was nothing false about him. What you saw is what you got.

Nathanael seemed like the ideal disciple. He was devoted to serving God and he had a stellar reputation. However, like all of us, he was not perfect. Nathanael was also a prejudiced man who was judgmental of others.

We see this after Philip told Nathanael that Jesus was from Nazareth. Nathanael responded, "Can anything good come out of Nazareth?"

Apparently, Nathanael was prejudiced against people from this town.

Nathanael felt he was better than the people of Nazareth. Of course, this was a pretty common feeling among the Jews from Jerusalem—they thought they were better than Jews from Nazareth.

Nazareth's people were kind of modern day rednecks. They were rough and rugged. They were loud and boisterous. They had a different accent than the Jews in Judea. Basically, Nathanael looked at people from Nazareth like a native New York City man would see a man from Hickville, USA. He looked down on them and judged them through his prejudiced eyes. He believed the common stereotype that Judean people were far superior to their Nazareth cousins. He was absolutely sure that the Messiah could not come from such a lowly place!

Had he allowed it, Nathaniel's prejudice could have kept him from getting in the game, becoming one of Jesus' disciples and playing a historic role in God's kingdom. Nathanael was being offered the chance of a lifetime—if he was willing to lay his preconceived notions aside.

Thankfully, Nathanael made the right choice, left everything, including his prejudice, behind and followed Jesus. As he spent time with Jesus allowing Jesus to change him, Nathanael became useful in God's kingdom.

As Nathanael walked daily with Jesus, he learned to overcome his prejudice. Here's the amazing thing about Nathanael: Even though he struggled with the same issue of prejudice in his heart as Jonah, he didn't let it sideline his Hall of Fame career. Instead, learning from Jesus, he overcame. Not only did he overcome his prejudice against fellow Jews that he thought were "less than" him, but he overcame prejudice against all people. After Jesus' ascension, tradition tells us that Nathanael became a missionary to the people of India, fulfilling Jesus' Great Commission to take the gospel to the ends of the earth.

It's funny—a man who struggled with prejudice against his fellow Jews overcame to such a degree that he was able to become a missionary even to the Gentiles! (Trust me, when he was sitting under the tree before he encountered Jesus, this was the absolute last thing that Nathanael ever thought was his destiny!)

Still, two thousand years later, when you research Nathanael, his Hall of Fame placard includes taking the gospel to India.

I don't know about you, but I want to follow Nathanael's example rather than Jonah's! I don't want to allow any form of prejudice to keep me from fulfilling God's plan for my life or accomplishing his purpose though me. I want to be remembered as an overcomer—a man who reached his potential—not someone who sat pouting on the sidelines because God didn't share his preconceived ideas and prejudice.

How do we do it?

Guys, we need to examine ourselves, face any areas of prejudice in our hearts, and repent. It is key to analyze when the prejudice began and what caused it. We must ask God to flood our hearts with love and respect for those we have been prejudiced against. Then we must begin anew showing the love of Jesus to everyone around us, especially those we once were prejudiced against. We need to begin today.

Dear heavenly Father, Please forgive me for all the times I have allowed prejudice into my heart. Forgive me for the bigoted way I treated _____. Help me to never allow a hint of prejudice in my life again. I want to become a man who shows love, compassion, and acceptance to all people, especially _____ who I have treated sinfully in the past.

*Please give me a supernatural, holy love for _____.
I never want to allow ugly prejudice inside my heart again. I want instead to demonstrate the love of Christ to a world of people in need of a Savior. Flood my heart with love and respect for those I have been prejudiced against.*

Thank you for pointing out this area of prejudice. Help me to totally destroy it. I never want to be prejudiced again. In Jesus' name, amen.

TRAINING DRILL

We discussed in this chapter how some churches are prejudiced against young people. Think about your church. Can you see ways that young people may feel unwelcome or unwanted in your church? Write them down, then ask God to give you a plan to fight against this so that they feel welcome, wanted, and loved.

TWO-A-DAYS

If your church has a group for young adults (i.e., older than the youth group, nineteen– to thirty-year-olds), volunteer to serve in this group. If your church doesn't have anything for this age group, start something and commit to loving and accepting this age group into your church.

TEAM MEETING

1. We all wrestle with some form of prejudice. What would be your area of prejudice?

2. We made the statement in this chapter that, "when we allow prejudice to have a place in our lives, we are giving ground to hatred." What do you think of this statement?

3. How does prejudice relate to the fact that young people are leaving the church?

4. What can you do about this?

5. What can we as a group do about it?

6. What stands out to you the most about Jonah's story? What did you learn from studying his game footage to help you avoid the trap he fell into in his life?

7. How can we as a group help you?

CHAPTER 11

PLAYING THROUGH DISAPPOINTMENT

Recently I read an article that listed the top twenty traitors in sports history. It was an interesting article, but the most interesting one was number one, from a sport I know very little about: soccer. However, the description that went with the winner's story was interesting.

The number one sports traitor was a man named Luis Figo. Apparently, Real Madrid and Barcelona are bitter rivals that meet several times each season and every match is a dramatic, exciting affair, kind of like when the Steelers play the Ravens or the Eagles play the Cowboys in the NFL.

That drama grew when Figo left Barcelona to join Real Madrid for a then-record 37.5 million pounds. When Figo returned to his old team's field for a game, he was showered with projectiles from the fans that once chanted his name. The following season, he won the La Liga title with Madrid and earned the Ballon D'Or award, which I am told is FIFA's equivalent of the NFL's MVP award. The hatred of Figo rose to new heights when Barça fans littered the field with debris that included a severed pig's head while he attempted to take a corner kick! They really hated this guy! In their eyes, he was a traitor.

No one likes a traitor! However, history is full of them.

I have always loved studying history, especially U.S. history. It is full of so many fascinating people. For example, if you were to study the American Revolution, you would learn about one of America's greatest generals. This man bravely fought to defeat the British at Ridgefield and Dansbury. He helped capture Fort Ticonderoga. He led the invasion of Canada. He used his own money to buy weapons and supplies for battle. He single-handedly rallied the troops at the Battle of Saratoga while enduring a crippling leg injury. This man was General Washington's most trusted officer. Without his leadership and military contributions, few believe we would have won our independence. Who is this general?

General Benedict Arnold.

Benedict Arnold is never remembered for any of his outstanding military achievements. Because he betrayed his country by attempting to sell West Point to the British, his name became synonymous with the most heinous acts of betrayal. This once great general is only remembered as a traitor to his country. What a sad waste of talent, ability, and potential!

The sad thing is the reason behind Benedict Arnold's betrayal. He became disappointed when he was passed over for a promotion.

His disappointment grew as other officers took credit for some of his military actions.

His disappointment increased when he was reprimanded by General Washington after a congressional inquiry into his actions in battle.

His disappointment with how he was being treated despite his great victories caused him to commit his terrible acts of treason. Instead of being remembered as a great military leader, he is known for heinous acts of treason. All because he allowed his disappointment to consume him.

Benedict Arnold was not the first leader to allow disappointment to destroy him.

The Bible gives us an excellent example of a man who had the world at his feet, but instead chose to abandon it all because of disappointment he faced. The story of Judas Iscariot, while one of the most well-known stories in the Bible, is also one of the saddest. However, it is also a stark reminder of the tremendous cost of allowing disappointment to rule our lives. Like Benedict Arnold, Judas could have had it all but threw it away because he allowed disappointment to consume him.

Almost everyone, whether a believer or unbeliever, knows the name Judas Iscariot. It has become synonymous with the word "traitor." Next to Benedict Arnold, he is probably the best-known traitor in history. But he didn't start out that way.

Judas was one of the twelve men hand-chosen by Jesus to be disciples. He was a first-round pick to be on Jesus' team. He went from living an obscure life to being one of the leaders of a new religious movement in Israel.

Judas had the extreme privilege of walking and talking with Jesus! Judas never met anyone like Jesus before. As an Israelite who lived under Roman oppression, Judas never felt hopeful about his future. But in Jesus he found hope, hope for a better life and a better future.

Judas saw in Jesus the long-awaited Messiah that would shake off the tyranny of the Romans and give freedom to the nation of Israel. Instead of being oppressed, Israel, and Judas as a head guy, would get to do the oppressing! Channeling his inner Lion King, Judas just couldn't wait to be king!

Judas was probably stoked when Jesus went into the temple, whip a-blazing, and told the religious leaders to shape up or ship out. In Judas' eyes, there was a new sheriff in town, and he was part of the posse. First they'd set the religious leaders straight, then on to the Romans!

However, things began to change. Jesus didn't immediately start a revolution. Instead of Jesus storming the Roman fortresses, he preached a message of love. Matthew 5 says:

"But I tell you, do not resist an evil person. If anyone slaps you on the right cheek, turn to them the other cheek also. And if anyone wants to sue you and take your shirt, hand over your coat as well. If anyone forces you to go one mile, go with them two miles. Give to the one who asks you, and do not turn away from the one who wants to borrow from you.

"You have heard that it was said, 'Love your neighbor and hate your enemy.' But I tell you, love your enemies and pray for those who persecute you, that you may be children of your Father in heaven."

This teaching must have floored Judas. When Jesus said to turn the other cheek when someone strikes you, or to go the extra mile, everyone in the crowd knew what he was referring to. The Roman soldiers were notorious for abusing the people of Israel and making them do forced labor. Instead of leading a revolt against the Romans, Jesus was teaching them to submit to their rule. This was *not* what Judas signed on for!

Over time, it became clear to Judas that Jesus had no intention of doing things the way he thought he would do them. Jesus' messages were about love, submission, and forgiveness, not revolution and anarchy. Instead of an immediate kingdom, Jesus spoke of a future kingdom. Judas must have been devastated to realize he gave up everything to follow Jesus into a revolt of the Roman Empire only to find that wasn't Jesus' plan.

Judas' disappointment in Jesus caused him to slowly drift away. Instead of following Jesus wholeheartedly, he started looking for ways to get something, anything, out of this deal. He wasn't willing to totally walk away; after all, Jesus was *the man* in Israel, and there was esteem in being part of the group. But he wasn't in it for the right reasons, and slowly, his heart began to turn. How do I know this? John 12 begins,

Six days before the Passover, Jesus came to Bethany, where Lazarus lived, whom Jesus had raised from the dead. Here a dinner was given in Jesus' honor. Martha served, while Lazarus was among those reclining at the table with him. Then Mary took about a pint of pure nard, an expensive perfume; she poured it on Jesus' feet and wiped his feet with her hair. And the house was filled with the fragrance of the perfume.

But one of his disciples, Judas Iscariot, who was later to betray him, objected, "Why wasn't this perfume sold and the money given to the poor? It was worth a year's wages." He did not say this because he cared about the poor but because he was a thief; as keeper of the money bag, he used to help himself to what was put into it.

You don't steal from someone you love and follow unconditionally! Judas reached a place where he decided he was going to get *something* out of this following Jesus thing. He still had a glimmer of hope that Jesus would come to his senses and lead the revolution that Judas felt he was destined to lead. Until then, he was going to put a little nest egg away for himself just in case.

Guys, disappointment has a way of making us feel that compromise is okay. Things aren't going the way we think they should go or the way we think we deserve, so we start to feel like we deserve to bend the rules or go against what we know is right. It deceives us into thinking we have a reason to sin; after all, if God did what he was suppose to do, we would never need to sin.

Judas's disappointment started him down a dangerous path. Before he knew it, he allowed his disappointment to destroy his relationship with Jesus. Let's look at Mark 14 beginning with verse 3.

While he was in Bethany, reclining at the table in the home of Simon the Leper, a woman came with an alabaster jar of very expensive perfume, made of pure nard. She broke the jar and poured the perfume on his head.

Some of those present were saying indignantly to one another, "Why this waste of perfume? It could have been sold for more than a year's wages and the money given to the poor." And they rebuked her harshly.

"Leave her alone," said Jesus. "Why are you bothering her? She has done a beautiful thing to me. The poor you will always have with you, and you can help them any time you want. But you will not always have me. She did what she could. She poured perfume on my body beforehand to prepare for my burial. Truly I tell you, wherever the gospel is preached throughout the world, what she has done will also be told, in memory of her."

Not again! Once again, a woman came to bless Jesus, once again she is reprimanded for wasting money, and once again Jesus took her side! Not only that, but instead of predicting a triumphant victory over Rome, Jesus was talking about his death being imminent. How did this second-verse-same-as-the-first incident make Judas feel?

Then Judas Iscariot, one of the Twelve, went to the chief priests to betray Jesus to them. They were delighted to hear this and promised to give him money. So he watched for an opportunity to hand him over.

Judas's disappointment with Jesus' ministry, actions, and teaching had reached its breaking point. He could not continue any longer. Jesus wasn't who he thought he was. He wasn't doing it Judas' way! His disappointment caused him to commit the ultimate betrayal: selling Jesus for the price of a common slave.

Honestly, I think there was a part of Judas, deep inside, that thought his actions were the helpful nudge Jesus needed. He was putting Jesus in a corner where Jesus would be forced to start the revolution. Whatever his reasoning, he made a decision that has lived in infamy ever since. All because he was disappointed in Jesus for not doing it the way he wanted him to do it. Matthew 27:1–5 says,

Early in the morning, all the chief priests and the elders of the people made their plans how to have Jesus executed. So they bound him, led him away and handed him over to Pilate the governor.

When Judas, who had betrayed him, saw that Jesus was condemned, he was seized with remorse and returned the thirty pieces of silver to the chief priests and the elders. "I have sinned," he said, "for I have betrayed innocent blood."

"What is that to us?" they replied. "That's your responsibility."

So Judas threw the money into the temple and left. Then he went away and hanged himself.

> **Judas just couldn't get past his disappointment that Jesus didn't do things his way.**

Judas' disappointment with God ended up destroying him! He was given the world when he was allowed to be Jesus' disciple, but his disappointment caused him to lose everything. He lost it all, hanging himself on a tree. What a sad ending to a life that held such promise. He just couldn't get past his disappointment that Jesus didn't do things his way.

Guys, disappointment will affect our relationship with God. Sometimes we think we have God figured out. We think we know exactly what he is going to do. We convince ourselves that our desires are really his will. Then when God does things differently than we expected, we get disappointed.

Judas demonstrated to each of us that disappointment can be a deadly weapon. We, too, can throw away a lifetime of promise because things don't work out the way we want.

- Our marriage isn't all fun, sex, and excitement. It comes with hard times, arguments, and struggles.
- The new job we wanted falls through our grasp and we find ourselves disappointed in God for not giving it to us.
- We don't receive the healing from God that we think we deserve.
- God doesn't bless our finances the way the preacher promised he would. We still struggle to make ends meet.

On and on the list goes. Life throws us a curveball, and God doesn't instantly jump in and save the day.

Life in God's kingdom doesn't turn out to be all candy canes and gumdrops, and we blame God.

We become disappointed that he didn't do what we thought he should do. This disappointment can cause us to do things we would never have dreamed of doing.

I will be honest with you: I have to be careful not to let disappointed with God creep back into my life. In my past, it's been a real struggle.

I am a dreamer by nature. I think about how I want God to work in my life. When God does things differently than I expect him to, I used to get disappointed and angry. This anger would get in the way of my relationship with God.

I remember once going to a service geared around healing. The speaker was a nationally known healing minister. Stories of people being healed were shown daily on his TV show. What they didn't show was the hundreds of people being brought to him in wheelchairs and hospital beds only to be wheeled back out at the end, still suffering physically. I went to this meeting convinced I would be healed of my disability, only to leave disappointed and angry.

I couldn't understand why God didn't heal me. I was devastated. I couldn't bring myself to share my feelings, and instead I buried them. However, the disappointment remained in me for years, turning into a bitter heart.

It was also around this time I started struggling with porn. I told myself it was no big deal, God owed me for not healing me. Like Judas, my disappointment twisted my thinking about sin, and it trapped me.

Eventually, God got through to me and made me face this heart issue. He lovingly but sternly showed me the sin I was committing against him. He helped me overcome my disappointment. He broke the strongholds it had developed in my life. Since then, I haven't touched pornography. Now I deal with disappointments differently.

I talk to God and confess my disappointment to him. I ask his forgiveness. Then I choose to accept whatever he chooses to do as his perfect will and go along with his program. I can't be angry at God for not doing what I wanted or envisioned in my mind. Instead, I must surrender my strong will and selfish desires to God and allow him to be in control.

Overcoming this trait is a mental battle.

I have to choose not to let my feelings control me. For instance, recently I attended a service, and the theme turned out to be on healing. At the end of the service, I left in the same pain as when I entered.

When the familiar feeling of disappointment started to creep back in, I had to take action. I had to decide not to let the feelings rule. Instead my mind had to rule.

I made a conscious decision to tell myself that God knows *way* more than I do. He knows why he allows me to continue suffering physically. He understands what he is using this pain to accomplish in my life. It is my job to go with it and let him do what he thinks is best, knowing, when it is his timing and will, he will heal me.

Judas wasn't the only person in history to deal with the opportunity to become disappointed with God. As a matter of fact, the Bible has an entire book dedicated to this particular issue.

> *Job was a man who lived in Uz. He was honest inside and out, a man of his word, who was totally devoted to God and hated evil with a passion. He had seven sons and three daughters. He was also very wealthy—seven thousand head of sheep, three thousand camels, five hundred teams of oxen, five hundred donkeys, and a huge staff of servants—the most influential man in all the East!* (Job 1:1–3, *The Message*)

The book of Job starts out telling us about the blessed life of a man named Job. Job had it all—wealth, esteem, property, a beautiful family, and God's blessing on his life. Fat City! But then one day, in order to show Satan that Job was the real deal and not just serving God for what he could get out of it, God allowed Satan to wipe Job clean.

In about an hour's time, Job lost EVERYTHING listed above.

Enemies attacked and stole his cattle, killing his servants in the process.

A freak lightning storm stuck and destroyed all of his sheep and livestock.

Simultaneously, a second enemy attacked and destroyed every camel he owned.

Amazingly, as all of this went on, a tornado came and destroyed the home where his children were all gathered, burying them dead in the rubble. What a horrible day!

If ever there was a man who should have been angry and disappointed in God, it was Job! What a horrible twenty-four hours! The Bible makes it clear: it all happened with God's permission. God chose to allow Job to lose everything! How did Job react?

At this, Job got up and tore his robe and shaved his head. Then he fell to the ground in worship and said: "Naked I came from my mother's womb, and naked I will depart. The LORD gave and the LORD has taken away; may the name of the LORD be praised."

In all this, Job did not sin by charging God with wrongdoing.

Wow! He never sinned against God! That is how you deal with life's disappointments! Judas allowed his disappointment to consume him and so he betrayed his friend and mentor. Job never entertained the idea of turning on God. Even when his own body was afflicted to the point of being near death, even when his friends and even his own wife turned on him and God, he never did.

Job is an excellent contrast to Judas on how a man of God handles disappointment. He refused to lose! In the end, his faithfulness was rewarded as God restored everything he had lost.

Guys, disappointment is a serious thing!

Benedict Arnold allowed disappointment to cause him to betray the colonial army.

Judas became disappointed with God and ended up backslidden and dead, hanging from a tree.

We must choose to be sons who submit to God and follow him wholeheartedly no matter where he leads. We need to trust that he knows more than us and will work things out for our good. This is the only way to receive God's blessing in our lives.

I hope you take this chapter seriously. Examine yourself to see if you have allowed disappointment with how God has done things in your life to cause you to turn away from him. Have feelings that you deserved better caused you to feel like you deserve to commit sins or do things you know you shouldn't do? If so, today is the day to turn things around!

Confess your sins to God.

Ask him to forgive you.

Repent of thinking you know better than him.

Ask him for the strength to trust his ways and his will.

Don't continue letting disappointment ruin your relationship with God.

Don't let it knock you out of the game.

Instead, run to God. He's waiting for you today.

Dear heavenly Father, please forgive me for allowing myself to be disappointed with you and the things you are doing in my life. Please forgive me for my arrogance in thinking I know better than you do or that you aren't doing things the way I want you to do them.

Help me to submit my will and desires to you and to trust that you have my best interest at heart. I do not want to continue allowing my disappointment to cause separation between you and me. Forgive me and strengthen me to do your will. In Jesus' name, amen.

TRAINING DRILL

We all face some form of disappointment in our lives. Looking back at your life, how did you react in your time of disappointment? Be honest with yourself and with God. Make a list of any sins or compromises you committed and ask God to forgive you.

TWO-A-DAYS

The best way to overcome disappointment is through exercising one thing—gratitude. Make a comprehensive list of things you can be grateful for. When disappointment rears its ugly head, use your gratitude list to combat it. You will be surprised how dwelling on things to be grateful for defeats feelings of disappointment.

TEAM MEETING

1. Have you ever been disappointed in how God did something in your life?

2. Have feelings that you deserved better caused you to feel like you deserve to commit sins or do things you know you shouldn't do?

3. Have you acted on your feelings?

4. Did you overcome your disappointment? If so, how?

5. What stands out to you the most about Judas' story? What did you learn from studying his game footage to help you avoid the trap he fell into in his life?

6. How can we as a group help you?

PART 4
BUILDING A
DYNASTY

CHAPTER 12

THE VALUE OF A GOOD COACH

I am a huge believer of the mentoring relationship! Guys, we are way better together than we are alone. History is full of epic bonds between two men.

- Moses and Joshua
- Jonathan and David
- Elijah and Elisha
- Peter and Mark
- Paul and Timothy
- The Lone Ranger and Tonto
- Batman and Robin
- Cory Matthews and Shawn Hunter (Okay, not epic, but *Boy Meets World* was huge when I was younger!)

God never intended man to go through life alone. His will is for the older men to take the wisdom and experience they gained and use it to help the younger men surpass them spiritually. It is all about working ourselves out of a job and helping the next generation thrive. It is the younger men's chance to humbly learn from another's mistakes, allowing them to avoid making the same mistakes as they grow into their own manhood. That's what it's all about.

Nothing is more beautiful to see than a healthy, thriving mentor–mentoree relationship. It is one of God's greatest gifts to man. Unfortunately, many men reject this gift from God, trading it in for things they think they want or need. What do I mean?

Well, the best way for me to explain is to look at the second-best guide for how to live life. Of course, the Bible is number one, the unchallenged source on how to live life. It teaches us everything we need to know for every area of life. The second place to learn about life is, of course, from the *Rocky* movies. John Wayne movies come in a close third, but Rocky gets the nudge in my opinion!

> **God never intended man to go through life alone. His will is for the older men to take the wisdom and experience they gained and use it to help the younger men surpass them spiritually.**

Recently, while thinking about how to write this chapter, I faced a really bad week. It started with someone crashing into my car and smashing the entire front end, and ended with me having a nasty flu. It was an awful week!

One night, unable to deal with one more thing, I flipped on the TV to just chill and relax for a bit. As I flipped around and around the channels at a breakneck speed looking for something to watch (C'mon, I am not the only one to sit and hold the channel button down!), I came across the gift that keeps on giving, a marathon of the *Rocky* movies! *Ka-ching!!*

The channel was showing *Rocky V.* Okay, I know, this is the one everyone said never should have been made, but, while it is not as good as the others, it still has a good lesson to it, and to be honest, I love the street fight at the end!

If you never saw the movie, first repent, and then I will tell you about it.

It picks up right where *Rocky IV* left off. Rocky has just defeated Ivan Drago (take that, communism!) and is the undisputed world champion and a national hero. However, the victory came at a huge cost. Steroid-enhanced Drago's severe beating of Rocky during the fight caused brain damage and vision loss. Rocky's days of fighting are over!

When he arrives home, things get worse. Oddly, his son had aged ten years during his short trip. His accountant had embezzled all of Rocky's wealth, leaving him broke. Having no money and unable to fight, Rocky moves back to the poor part of Philly. All he owns in the world is Mick's old gym. So Rocky opens the gym and starts training fighters.

He ends up training a fighter who has the cheesiest movie name ever, Tommy Gunn. Rocky decides he is going to be Mick to Tommy—he would mentor him and train him to fight, teaching Tommy everything he needed to know to become the champ. What an amazing opportunity! Any fighter would kill for this chance, right?

Wrong! Tommy stupidly walks away from Rocky to chase after fame and fortune with another promoter. However, this promoter doesn't care about Tommy. Rocky had taken Tommy in, let him live with his family, and given him some of the little they had. He taught him everything he knew about fighting and trained him to be the next great champion. Tommy had the chance of a lifetime to have the greatest boxing mentor relationship ever (something Adonis Creed took full advantage of many years later), but he traded it for greed and fame. What an idiot!

Tommy Gunn was not the first man to trade a dream mentorship to chase after what he thought he wanted. The Bible tells us the story of the original Tommy Gunn, a man who had the dream mentor relationship from God, but traded it away for something he thought was more important. His story is a fabulous warning against asking God if he kept the receipt when he gives us the great gift of a mentor. Let's look at the life of Gehazi.

Gehazi's story is found directly after one of my favorite mentor stories in the Bible. If you read my book *Legacy: Living a Life that Lasts,* you know how much I love the relationship of Elijah and Elisha.

Elijah chose Elisha to enter into a mentor relationship with him. 2 Kings 2 tells the beautiful story of how God called Elijah to heaven and how Elisha refused to leave his beloved mentor until Elijah blessed him and gave him a double portion of his spirit. What an awesome request!

God heard Elisha's request, and he gave him the double portion to Elisha. As a matter of fact, in the Bible, Elijah performed seven amazing miracles, and it shows us Elisha performed exactly fourteen, double what Elijah performed, aka the double portion.

Elisha was *the man* in the Old Testament. He became a legend through the power of God, judging bratty kids who hated bald men via a hungry bear, making metal float, turning a bottle of oil into an oil factory that supplied oil to a whole town, and even raising people from the dead! The dude had the power of God on his life!

Elisha decided that he was going to choose a mentor just like Elijah had done for him. So he chooses a young man named Gehazi.

Ka-ching! Gehazi hit the jackpot!

He was given the chance to learn and be mentored by the greatest prophet to ever live. If he was faithful and loyal, he might receive a double portion of Elisha's spirit just like Elisha had received from his mentor! He could learn under the best and hopefully one day surpass his mentor, as the mentor relationship requires.

However, Gehazi was no Elisha. Eventually his inner Tommy Gunn came out, and he made a foolish decision. Let's look at 2 Kings 5.

Now Naaman was commander of the army of the king of Aram.
He was a great man in the sight of his master and highly regarded,
because through him the LORD had given victory to Aram.

This passage introduces us to a man named Naaman. Naaman was
one bad dude! Think someone like the Rock or Vin Diesel. He was a
guy you didn't want to mess with! He was a commander in one of the
greatest powers of his day, Aram.

Aram was one of the countries God used to punish Israel for their
sins against him. The passage clearly says he was a military force and
had God's hand of favor on his life. Lucky dude, right?

He was a valiant soldier, but he had leprosy.

Ouch! Leprosy was the worst disease someone could have in bibli-
cal times. It literally ate you alive. It devoured body parts, rotting them
off. What an awful disease to have, especially for a soldier. Think about
it: he could be in a sword fight, swing his sword at someone, and have
his arm fly off! His life, especially his military career, was numbered as
he received this death sentence!

Now bands of raiders from Aram had gone out and had taken cap-
tive a young girl from Israel, and she served Naaman's wife. She
said to her mistress, "If only my master would see the prophet who
is in Samaria! He would cure him of his leprosy."

Who was this prophet? You guessed it, Elisha! His fame was known
far and wide as the man with God's power. He had already raised a
man from the dead; curing leprosy would be a piece of cake for him!

Naaman went to his master and told him what the girl from Israel
had said. "By all means, go," the king of Aram replied. "I will send
a letter to the king of Israel." So Naaman left, taking with him ten
talents of silver, six thousand shekels of gold and ten sets of clothing.
The letter that he took to the king of Israel read: "With this letter I

am sending my servant Naaman to you so that you may cure him of his leprosy."

As soon as the king of Israel read the letter, he tore his robes and said, "Am I God? Can I kill and bring back to life? Why does this fellow send someone to me to be cured of his leprosy? See how he is trying to pick a quarrel with me!"

Okay, the king of Israel was an evil man who had led Israel into sin and eventually under the rule of conquering Aram, but still, you have to feel for the guy! Imagine getting a letter from a mad dictator saying, "This is my top guy, he's dying, fix him!"

I get his response! Apparently, so did Elisha.

When Elisha the man of God heard that the king of Israel had torn his robes, he sent him this message: "Why have you torn your robes? Have the man come to me and he will know that there is a prophet in Israel." So Naaman went with his horses and chariots and stopped at the door of Elisha's house. Elisha sent a messenger to say to him, "Go, wash yourself seven times in the Jordan, and your flesh will be restored and you will be cleansed."

That's an odd prescription! Go for a swim in the Jordan, and you will be good to go. Seems too easy, right? That's exactly what Naaman thought.

But Naaman went away angry and said, "I thought that he would surely come out to me and stand and call on the name of the LORD his God, wave his hand over the spot and cure me of my leprosy. Are not Abana and Pharpar, the rivers of Damascus, better than all the waters of Israel? Couldn't I wash in them and be cleansed?" So he turned and went off in a rage.

Naaman was ticked! He expected something more grandiose than this prescription. Remember, this man was a military powerhouse. He was not a man you wanted to make angry!

Naaman's servants went to him and said, "My father, if the prophet had told you to do some great thing, would you not have done it? How much more, then, when he tells you, 'Wash and be cleansed'!" So he went down and dipped himself in the Jordan seven times, as the man of God had told him, and his flesh was restored and became clean like that of a young boy.

Luckily, Naaman had someone around him strong enough to speak the truth and reason with him. As a result, Naaman was healed. It said he was restored to the flesh of a young boy. He not only got healed, but lost a few years of aging to boot! Put another notch on Elisha's miracle belt!

"Great story Jamie, but what does it have to do with Gehazi and mentoring?"

I am glad you asked. Let's pick up Gehazi's part in the next verses.

Then Naaman and all his attendants went back to the man of God. He stood before him and said, "Now I know that there is no God in all the world except in Israel. So please accept a gift from your servant."

The prophet answered, "As surely as the Lord lives, whom I serve, I will not accept a thing." And even though Naaman urged him, he refused.

"If you will not," said Naaman, "please let me, your servant, be given as much earth as a pair of mules can carry, for your servant will never again make burnt offerings and sacrifices to any other god but the Lord. But may the Lord forgive your servant for this one thing: When my master enters the temple of Rimmon to bow down and he is leaning on my arm and I have to bow there also—

when I bow down in the temple of Rimmon, may the LORD forgive your servant for this."

"Go in peace," Elisha said.

Naaman was thrilled to be healed, and he wanted to repay Elisha for this tremendous blessing. Elisha basically said, "Keep it, give God the glory, not me!" He refused any gifts, and Naaman went on his way.

Meanwhile, Gehazi stood in the background watching this whole scene. He eyes must have bugged out when he saw the wealth that Naaman offered his boss. Welcome to Fat City! This internship thing was finally gonna pay off!

I wonder how many bugs Gehazi swallowed as his mouth hung open from shock when Elisha refused the gift. He was stunned at Elisha! He was sure Elisha was wrong and didn't know what he was doing. He decided he was going to fix it.

After Naaman had traveled some distance, Gehazi, the servant of Elisha the man of God, said to himself, "My master was too easy on Naaman, this Aramean, by not accepting from him what he brought. As surely as the LORD lives, I will run after him and get something from him."

So Gehazi hurried after Naaman. When Naaman saw him running toward him, he got down from the chariot to meet him. "Is everything all right?" he asked.

"Everything is all right," Gehazi answered. "My master sent me to say, 'Two young men from the company of the prophets have just come to me from the hill country of Ephraim. Please give them a talent of silver and two sets of clothing.'"

"By all means, take two talents," said Naaman. He urged Gehazi to accept them, and then tied up the two talents of silver in two bags, with two sets of clothing. He gave them to two of his servants, and they carried them ahead of Gehazi. When Gehazi came to the

hill, he took the things from the servants and put them away in the house. He sent the men away and they left.

Gehazi couldn't say no. He had to have the blessings Naaman offered, no matter what it took. So he snuck away, lied, and then hid the gifts. He thought he had it made. What he didn't realize was the same God that performed the miracles through Elisha could tell Elisha what Gehazi had done.

When he went in and stood before his master, Elisha asked him, "Where have you been, Gehazi?"

"Your servant didn't go anywhere," Gehazi answered.

Yeah, lying to a prophet always works, right? He makes Tommy Gunn look like Einstein!

But Elisha said to him, "Was not my spirit with you when the man got down from his chariot to meet you? Is this the time to take money or to accept clothes—or olive groves and vineyards, or flocks and herds, or male and female slaves? Naaman's leprosy will cling to you and to your descendants forever." Then Gehazi went from Elisha's presence and his skin was leprous—it had become as white as snow.

Wow, Gehazi lost it all! He was given the gift from God of being mentored and trained by *the* man of God of his time, and he instead traded it in for two big hunks of silver and some new jeans.

He could have had it all, but he traded it for what he wanted, and he lost it all. Instead of being the next great prophet of Israel and performing twenty-eight miracles to Elisha's fourteen, he spent the remainder of his life littering body parts in a leper colony. Guys, we can't make this same mistake.

"Jamie, I would never trade the blessing of a mentor for two pair of jeans!"

You're probably right. But every day, men choose to exchange the privilege of being mentored for other things.

- Some won't be mentored because they refuse to be teachable.
- Others refuse to be vulnerable, to be open and honest about themselves.
- Some keep sins hidden from their mentor instead of allowing their mentors to know and help them.
- Others won't make time in their schedule to spend with a mentor.
- Still others are too proud to even admit they need another man's help and guidance.

There are lots of ways to reject God's gift of a mentor. Unfortunately, many men are choosing to do this. They won't enter into any kind of mentoring relationship. Many others refuse to use this gift to the fullest extent they can. Guys, this should not be so!

God's design and plan is what we saw with Elijah and Elisha, not with Elisha and Gehazi. God wants his men to learn and glean everything we can from each other. He wants us to strive to outdo our mentors because we avoid the pitfalls they experienced. We are to learn everything we possibly can so we can become all God created us to be. Our mentors should invest everything they have in us, and we, in turn, look to pour it all into other men so they can surpass us spiritually.

> **God wants his men to learn and glean everything we can from each other. He wants us to strive to outdo our mentor because we avoid the pitfalls they experienced. We are to strive to learn everything we possibly can so we can become all God created us to be.**

Elisha did this. He did twice as many things for God as Elijah had done, and then he worked to set up Gehazi so that Gehazi could surpass him spiritually. Unfortunately, Gehazi broke the cycle, and instead of performing twenty-eight miracles and training another man to perform fifty-six miracles in the future, he spent the rest of his life thinking it was a miracle if he ended the day with as many fingers and toes as he woke up with that morning. Such a sad portrait of failed discipleship, all because he wanted something other than spiritual growth and therefore didn't submit to his mentor.

Gehazi, like Tommy Gunn but to a greater and more serious degree, shows us the cost of not appreciating and taking advantage of a mentor relationship. Their stories should cause us to evaluate ourselves and ask some serious questions.

- Am I even involved in a mentor relationship?
- Am I being teachable and submissive?
- Am I holding back anything in this relationship?
- Am I humble enough to be mentored?
- Do I allow other things to take precedence over my mentor relationship?

These are great questions to ask yourself. If your answers are not all positive, I encourage you to do two things.

First, ask God to forgive you. Repent for taking his blessing of a mentor for granted, and ask him to change your heart so you can take full advantage of this amazing opportunity of having another man influence your life.

Then, go to your mentor and ask him to forgive you. Tell him you are sorry for taking advantage of his time. Tell him you are going to commit yourself wholeheartedly to his guidance. Ask him to test you and see that you're serious. Then commit to the relationship 100 percent, holding nothing back.

A mentor truly is a gift from God. We can't continue coughing up the ball that our veteran quarterback hands to us. We must learn from Ghazi the tremendous cost of rejecting a mentoring relationship, failing to become all we can become in God's kingdom. If you don't have a mentor, actively seek one out.

If you have a mentor, learn all you can from his successes and his failures, and become an even greater asset to your team—the kingdom of God.

Embracing mentorship—it's a key component to getting in and winning the game of life.

Dear heavenly Father, thank you so much for allowing me the tremendous gift of having a mentor. Father, please forgive me if I have been taking this relationship for granted or have been holding back. I truly see the need for this relationship; help me to commit myself wholeheartedly to it.

Father, help me to surrender all pride, fear, or insecurities that are keeping me from being completely open. Help me to be willing to sacrifice my time and/or desires so I can glean all I can from my mentor. Help me learn from him so I can avoid pitfalls he took in life. Allow our time together to mold me into the man you want me to be. Thank you for this amazing gift; help me take full advantage of this opportunity. In Jesus' name, amen.

TRAINING DRILL

If you are not currently in a mentoring relationship, immediately seek out a mentor in your life.

If you have a mentor, ask him to forgive you for anytime you didn't embrace his wisdom and advice.

TWO-A-DAYS

Ask your mentor the questions we listed at the end of the chapter and accept his responses to you. Reaffirm to him your commitment to the mentoring relationship and your willingness to change.

TEAM MEETING

1. Do you have a mentor? How did you meet?

2. Why is it a good thing to have a mentor?

3. This chapter listed some ways men struggle to take full advantage of a mentor relationship. What is your biggest struggle?

4. How can you overcome this struggle?

5. What is your biggest fear about being mentored?

6. Is this a rational fear? What can you do to overcome?

7. What stands out to you the most about Gehazi's story? What did you learn from studying his game footage to help you avoid the trap he fell into in his life?

8. How can we as a group work together to encourage mentorship?

9. Is there a man you can be a mentor to?

CHAPTER 13

BEING A TEAM PLAYER

Let me ask you a question. If you got hit in the head and had a concussion, do you have someone you could call and ask to stay up with you to keep you awake?

I can hear you saying, "Wow Jamie, where did that come from? What a weird question!"

I am not crazy. Let me show you where we are going with this question.

Once, I was watching a show on TV where a man was playing football. He was a forty-something-year-old man in great shape. Being a little too cocky, he relied on his good physique to help him play ball with kids half his age. However, he found out on the first play that he wasn't as young as he used to be!

Playing quarterback, he called for the snap. The ball came to him in the shotgun formation, and two seconds later a huge linebacker obliterated him, knocking him out cold! After waking up, he had a concussion. As is always the case with head concussions, the doctors told him to stay awake for twenty-four hours to make sure there were no complications.

Well, this man's wife was out of town, and his kids were young and couldn't stay awake to make sure he stayed awake. How was this injured, tired guy ever going to follow the doctor's orders?

As he sat on his sofa struggling to stay awake, he heard a knock at the door. It was three of his friends, pizza in hand, arriving to help their friend stay awake through the night.

I instantly thought, "That's what it's all about! Men helping men and being there for each other, not only in the good times, but the bad!" Thus my question, if you got hit in the head and had a concussion, do you have someone you could call and ask to stay up with you to keep you awake?

Guys, we need to have other men in our lives. No man is an island! We can't Lone Ranger our way through life. Heck, the Lone Ranger didn't even fly solo; he had Tonto!

Our teammates supply support to us. They provide a way for us to have accountability in our lives.

We need men in our lives. We need teammates, what some refer to as a spiritual band of brothers. Why?

Our teammates supply support to us. They provide a way for us to have accountability in our lives. We all need to be accountable to each other.

Our band of brothers are men we can trust to look us in the eye and say, "Your priorities are out of whack."

They can say to us, "Bro, you need to make a change here."

They are men we are completely open with who can ask us anything they want.

A few years back, a good friend of mine went through a very difficult time, and unfortunately this friend became very bitter. Over time, the anger and bitterness became like a poison, contaminating everyone who came in contact with this person.

This friend's behavior began to really affect me. I started to struggle to follow God down certain paths he was leading me. I began looking at certain people through my bitter friend's eyes, not God's eyes. I was sinking fast.

One of my teammates and his wife kindly confronted me and showed me that I was in trouble. They helped me see how this friend's bitterness was affecting me, and they lovingly pointed me away from this mindset and back to what God had called me to do.

This is what it is all about: men helping men. Such men help us grow in our walk with God. They point out areas of sin in us, help us see it, and encourage us to grow and overcome!

Peter had such a friend. The Bible tells us that Peter was a man who loved to eat ham! Peter was a bacon guy just like me! However, a good Jew didn't dare eat bacon, so when Peter was around Jews, he acted like he hated pork, but when he was around Gentiles, it was BLTs and chips nonstop.

Paul loved Peter enough to pull him aside and show him that this was sin.

Galatians 2:11–14 (*The Message*) says,

Later, when Peter came to Antioch, I had a face-to-face confrontation with him because he was clearly out of line. Here's the situation. Earlier, before certain persons had come from James, Peter regularly ate with the non-Jews. But when that conservative group came from Jerusalem, he cautiously pulled back and put as much distance as he could manage between himself and his non-Jewish friends. That's how fearful he was of the conservative Jewish clique that's been pushing the old system of circumcision. Unfortunately, the rest of the Jews in the Antioch church joined in that hypocrisy so that even Barnabas was swept along in the charade.

But when I saw that they were not maintaining a steady, straight course according to the Message, I spoke up to Peter in front of them all: "If you, a Jew, live like a non-Jew when you're not being observed by the watchdogs from Jerusalem, what right do you have to require non-Jews to conform to Jewish customs just to make a favorable impression on your old Jerusalem cronies?" (The Message)

We need such men in our lives, men who will point out areas of sin and show us what we need to change. We also need them so we have someone to reach out to in times of trouble. When the going gets tough, we need men in our lives we can cry out to and say, "I am in a battle, I need help! Will you fight with me?"

Jesus did this while in earth. On the night he knew he would be betrayed, he took his three closest friends aside and asked them to support him. Matthew 26:36–38,

Then Jesus went with his disciples to a place called Gethsemane, and he said to them, "Sit here while I go over there and pray." He took Peter and the two sons of Zebedee along with him, and he began to be sorrowful and troubled. Then he said to them, "My soul is overwhelmed with sorrow to the point of death. Stay here and keep watch with me."

Jesus knew what he would face that night, and he wanted his closest friends to help him get through it.

Paul also looked for men to come alongside of him during his times of trial. Throughout the book of Acts, we see Paul constantly surrounding himself with men who helped him through the hard times he faced. When facing his darkest hour, awaiting his death at the hands of an insane dictator, Nero, he reached out to his friends to support him.

2 Timothy 4:9–11 says, *"Do your best to come to me quickly, …Only Luke is with me. Get Mark and bring him with you, because he is helpful to me in my ministry."*

Facing a time of trial, Paul wanted to gather his men around him for help and support.

I seriously don't know what I would do without my band of brothers. Just a few weeks ago, I was facing a really tough situation, and I honestly didn't know which way to go. I immediately dropped an email to my guys, asked for support and prayer, and literally within a minute, my phone rang. It was one of my boys calling to help me.

Over the next few days, these men held me up in prayer, and I could literally feel their prayers making a difference. This is the reason we need a band of brothers.

We need men around us whom we can learn from. We gain prayer support and encouragement from our teammates.

Recently, I was on the road for a Mantour Conference, and I was scheduled to lead a very intense and heavy workshop. The night before as I lay in my hotel bed, I could not fall asleep. I watched as the clocked changed from midnight to 1 a.m., then to 2 a.m., then to 3. Finally, around 3:30 a.m., I fell asleep.

The next day I woke up to see a message on my iPhone. One of my friends had sent me a message at 3:30 a.m. saying God woke him up and had him praying for me. He started praying at the exact time I was able to fall asleep. Thanks to this teammate's obedience to God, I fell asleep, and, a few hours later, led the workshop. *That's* why we need teammates, men who can hold us up and support us.

We can all learn from each other. There is no trial or temptation that is new under the sun, and it is time for God's men to be open and vulnerable and admit to our struggles and weaknesses so we can support each other, but also learn from others how to gain victories or avoid defeats. A band of brothers can help each other by saying, "I struggled with this area, I learned this going through it, now here is how you avoid making the same mistake."

I have a friend who is starting the road to ministry. His journey is very similar to the journey God took me on many years ago. God has allowed me to help encourage him and give him help and advice. I have been able to help him avoid some of the mistakes I made. I have been able to give him guidance as to what path to take or what decisions to make based on my own personal experiences. I don't say this to make myself look good. I say it to show how God can use us. Why should this man have to strive and struggle when I have gone through the same thing?

I have had other guys do the same for me. I remember once when I had an opportunity to try a type of outreach that I hadn't done before. This was a *huge* opportunity for me. The man who invited me, a good friend of mine, sat in on my outreach. Half-way through, he came up front and began co-teaching with me. I was honestly shocked and instantly I thought, "Wow, I blew it! He didn't like how I handled this situation, and he took it over."

I was crushed. I felt like I blew a big opportunity. I felt like a failure. I didn't get a chance to talk to this guy after the meeting as we both were mobbed with men asking us questions, but late that night, he called me on the phone. He explained to me what had happened.

> **THAT is what it's all about: men helping men, showing other men what you learned on your journey into manhood.**

He said he always intended to interrupt and take part in the class because he wanted to help me learn. He then went on to show how he had orchestrated everything about the outreach, the crowd size, the topic, everything, so that I would succeed and also learn from him for future events. I went from feeling like a failure to feeling loved and protected by a father-like figure.

I will never, ever forget how this man invested in me and made sure I learned and grew in a safe environment, while giving me a chance to grow and succeed. He poured into me what he had learned over the years, just like I am pouring into this friend of mine as he goes down the path of ministry. THAT is what it is all about: men helping men, showing other men what you learned on your journey into manhood.

We all need this in our lives. We need to work together and help each other on this journey along the Christian life.

What about you?

Who are your teammates?

Do you have a band of brothers?

Who are the men in your life who are investing in you, showing you ways to avoid the same mistakes and failures they encountered?

Do you have men you can contact for help when going through tough times?

Are there men in your life who will love you enough to stare you straight in the eyes and say, "Bro, you're in trouble. Stop what you are doing"?

We all need men in our lives like this. If you don't have such men in your life, start asking God to send them. Start attending a Bible-believing church. You will connect with other believers who can disciple you and help you along your spiritual journey. You will meet younger guys you can invest in as they grow in God.

If you are not already attending a men's group, I recommend you connect with the one at your church. If your church doesn't have a men's ministry, contact me and I'll help you get one started.

None of us were meant to live this life alone. Just as even the greatest football player in the world can't win the game without his teammates, we can't become all God wants us to be unless we are part of a team.

It's the way God designed it—are you willing to become a team player?

TRAINING DRILL

Make a list of your teammates. Think of three ways each man has helped you grow in your walk with God. Then send each of them a note thanking them.

TWO-A-DAYS

Find a guy at your church who hasn't really connected yet and make him one of your teammates. That way you and the rest of the guys on your team can help him feel like he belongs and has a place in the church family.

TEAM MEETING

1. "No man is an island." What does this statement mean to you?

2. Does the thought of having men in your life who can ask you anything or hold you accountable freak you out? Why?

3. Who is someone who has invested in your life?

4. How has his investment benefited you?

5. Who is a new man at your church you and your group can reach out to and include onto your team?

6. What stands out to you the most about Peter and Paul's story? What did you learn from studying their game footage to help you?

7. How can we as a group help you?

CHAPTER 14

BUILDING THE TEAM FOR THE FUTURE

Have you ever seen the show *American Ninja Warrior*?

I love this show. If you have never seen it, it's a reality show where people run through an overwhelmingly hard obstacle course that requires pure, brute strength and athleticism to get through each obstacle. The goal is to make it to the finale, a chance to try and conquer the infamous "Mount Midoriyama," an insane obstacle course that, at the time of this writing, only two have ever completed.

One aspect of the show I love is the camaraderie of the contestants. They are like brothers. They cheer each other on as they all run the course. The competition is with the course, not each other, and they want to push each other to be the best "ninja" they can be. While they all want to conquer the course, the goal is defeating the obstacles, and they don't care who does it!

Recently, I watched one of the qualifying rounds. This course was brutal. No one was finishing it. No one was climbing the last obstacle and hitting the buzzer. Veteran after veteran failed. Then a new ninja took the course.

This young new ninja attacked the course, methodically conquering each and every element. At the end of his run, he was the first to make it all the way to the top.

What stood out to me the most about his run was not his effort, but the reaction of all the other guys who had run the course before him.

They could have been jealous that he outdid them.

They could have booed or badmouthed him. But they didn't.

They walked along each obstacle, shouting encouragement and cheering him on. When he began to struggle, they shouted encouragement that he could do it. And when he reached the top of the last obstacle and hit the buzzer, they all celebrated as if they had been the ones who finished the course.

As I watched this, I screamed inside, "That is how it needs to be in God's kingdom! We need to stop having turf wars and stop making sure everyone knows our successes. We can't keep holding people back to make sure we hang onto our area of ministry or service. Instead we need to set the bar for the next generation to shoot for, and then scream and holler encouragement at them as they strive to go even further in God's kingdom. Then we need to celebrate like crazy when they reach the goals we were unable to achieve!"

That is our calling in life. We need to realize that our generation's ceiling is the next generation's floor. We need to give the younger men an example to try and surpass, and then we need to celebrate with them when they surpass us. It's how we continue the legacy of godliness.

"My generation's ceiling is the next generation's floor."

I love this quote. In my opinion this should be the definition of mentorship.

This is the attitude all men of God should adopt in their lives. We should encourage the next generation to surpass us spiritually! We should never discourage them in order to promote ourselves and our interests. A real man of God hopes the next generation goes above and beyond what he is doing and then does all he can to help them do it!

That is what we will look at as we work through this final chapter together. We will see an excellent example of a man who knew how to help the next generation realize that his ceiling could be their floor, their launching pad for success.

Who is this man? It is King David.

I love David. He was a passionate man! Sometimes that passion got him into trouble, sometimes it produced amazing results, but he never did anything half-heartedly!

Most know David as the man who killed Goliath with a slingshot and a stone. However, the part of his life we will look at comes toward the end of his life.

David had gone through years of living as a wanted man while King Saul tried to capture and kill him. He has now been made king of Israel, and instead of sleeping on a rock floor in a cave, he sleeps in a royal palace, living in the blessing of God's promises fulfilled. Let's look at 2 Samuel 7 beginning with verse 1 (NKJV):

> Now it came to pass when the king was dwelling in his house, and the LORD had given him rest from all his enemies all around, that the king said to Nathan the prophet, "See now, I dwell in a house of cedar, but the ark of God dwells inside tent curtains."
>
> Then Nathan said to the king, "Go, do all that is in your heart, for the LORD is with you."

David, grateful to God for all he has done to bless his life, wants to show his gratitude by building a grand temple to God. The prophet gave his blessing for the project, but unfortunately, neither David nor Nathan checked in with God before filing for the building permit.

> But it happened that night that the word of the LORD came to Nathan, saying, "Go and tell My servant David, 'Thus says the

Lord: "Would you build a house for Me to dwell in? For I have not dwelt in a house since the time that I brought the children of Israel up from Egypt, even to this day, but have moved about in a tent and in a tabernacle. ...Now therefore, thus shall you say to My servant David, 'Thus says the LORD of hosts: "I took you from the sheepfold, from following the sheep, to be ruler over My people, over Israel. And I have been with you wherever you have gone, and have cut off all your enemies from before you, and have made you a great name, like the name of the great men who are on the earth. Moreover I will appoint a place for My people Israel, and will plant them, that they may dwell in a place of their own and move no more; nor shall the sons of wickedness oppress them anymore, as previously, since the time that I commanded judges to be over My people Israel, and have caused you to rest from all your enemies. Also the LORD tells you that He will make you a house.

"When your days are fulfilled and you rest with your fathers, I will set up your seed after you, who will come from your body, and I will establish his kingdom. He shall build a house for My name, and I will establish the throne of his kingdom forever. I will be his Father, and he shall be My son. If he commits iniquity, I will chasten him with the rod of men and with the blows of the sons of men. But My mercy shall not depart from him, as I took it from Saul, whom I removed from before you. And your house and your kingdom shall be established forever before you. Your throne shall be established forever."

God tells David that he was not to build a temple for him. It was not God's will or timing. However, God says that in the future, he will allow another man, a younger man, a successor, one of David's sons, to build him a temple. That man was Solomon, the same Solomon we discussed earlier in this book.

Now, David has a decision to make here. He can either accept what God says and go with it, realizing his ceiling in life has been set by God and do what he can to help the next king soar above and beyond him, or he can pout and sulk because he will be outdone and surpassed by another.

What decision did David make?

Let's look at 1 Chronicles 22 (NKJV), and as we do we will see lessons we can learn to help us help younger men surpass us in God's kingdom.

1. DAVID SET SOLOMON UP TO SUCCEED

Then David said, "This is the house of the LORD God, and this is the altar of burnt offering for Israel." So David commanded to gather the aliens who were in the land of Israel; and he appointed masons to cut hewn stones to build the house of God. And David prepared iron in abundance for the nails of the doors of the gates and for the joints, and bronze in abundance beyond measure, and cedar trees in abundance; for the Sidonians and those from Tyre brought much cedar wood to David.

Now David said, "Solomon my son is young and inexperienced, and the house to be built for the LORD must be exceedingly magnificent, famous and glorious throughout all countries. I will now make preparation for it." So David made abundant preparations before his death.

David didn't pout about God's decision. He didn't rebel and disobey God. He didn't try to undermine Solomon or make it harder to protect his legacy. He did the opposite.

He realized his son was young and inexperienced, so he did everything in his power to make the project easier for Solomon.

God told him he couldn't build the temple, but he never said he couldn't plan it, stockpile for it, and gather a reliable workforce to ensure Solomon succeeded.

David realized an important point we all need to learn: **The work was about God's kingdom, not personal accomplishment. As long as the work gets done and the kingdom grows, who cares who gets the credit!**

It's not about us, it's about God's kingdom.

And guess what: no matter how hard you may try to outdo others in ministry, if it is God's will for them to outdo you, you won't be able to stop it. So get out of their way, get behind them, and do what you can to advance God's will.

2. DAVID TAUGHT SOLOMON HOW TO SUCCEED

The work was about God's kingdom, not personal accomplishment. As long as the work gets done and the kingdom grows, who cares who gets the credit!

1 Chronicles 28:9–19 says:

"As for you, my son Solomon, know the God of your father, and serve Him with a loyal heart and with a willing mind; for the LORD searches all hearts and understands all the intent of the thoughts. If you seek Him, He will be found by you; but if you forsake Him, He will cast you off forever. Consider now, for the LORD has chosen you to build a house for the sanctuary; be strong, and do it."

Then David gave his son, Solomon, the plans for the vestibule, its houses, its treasuries, its upper chambers, its inner chambers, and the place of the mercy seat; and the plans for all that he had by the

Spirit, of the courts of the house of the LORD, of all the chambers all around, of the treasuries of the house of God, and of the treasuries for the dedicated things; also for the division of the priests and the Levites, for all the work of the service of the house of the LORD, and for all the articles of service in the house of the LORD. He gave gold by weight for things of gold, for all articles used in every kind of service; also silver for all articles of silver by weight, for all articles used in every kind of service; the weight for the lampstands of gold, and their lamps of gold, by weight for each lampstand and its lamps; for the lampstands of silver by weight, for the lampstand and its lamps, according to the use of each lampstand. And by weight he gave gold for the tables of the showbread, for each table, and silver for the tables of silver; also pure gold for the forks, the basins, the pitchers of pure gold, and the golden bowls—he gave gold by weight for every bowl; and for the silver bowls, silver by weight for every bowl; and refined gold by weight for the altar of incense, and for the construction of the chariot, that is, the gold cherubim that spread their wings and overshadowed the ark of the covenant of the LORD. "All this," said David, "the LORD made me understand in writing, by His hand upon me, all the works of these plans."

David laid it all out for Solomon. He told him about God's command for his life and Solomon's life. He showed him the plan he had made but was unable to carry out. Then he showed him all the outlines and blueprints and all the tools and supplies he had prepared. Solomon was set to succeed, and David taught him how to do it.

Solomon was truly blessed to have such a man in his life. A man with David's attitude is hard to find. Many men take the attitude that they are not going to help their successor outdo them. Whether it be an out-and-out defiance or a tamer, more passive-aggressive feeling of "I learned a lot doing it the hard way, I wouldn't want to deprive them of this experience," men leave the next generation high and dry to ensure they don't get outdone. My brothers, this should not be so!

Instead, we should do anything and everything we can to help them succeed. I have a friend who models this to me all the time. He has a position of authority in ministry, but he understands that he is only one man and can only do so much. Instead of holding other men like myself down, he lets us loose to minister, he coaches us as we go, and he teaches us what we need to do to succeed.

He realizes it is about more than him; it is about advancing the kingdom, and as long as that gets done, he will let others do it. Such a man is a gem, and unfortunately, hard to find. However, it is the type of attitude each of us needs to develop into in our lives.

3. DAVID GATHERED OTHERS TO HELP SOLOMON SUCCEED

In 1 Chronicles 22:17–19 (NKJV), David also commanded all the leaders of Israel to help Solomon, saying, *"Is not the LORD your God with you? And has He not given you rest on every side? For He has given the inhabitants of the land into my hand, and the land is subdued before the LORD and before His people. Now set your heart and your soul to seek the LORD your God. Therefore arise and build the sanctuary of the LORD God, to bring the ark of the covenant of the LORD and the holy articles of God into the house that is to be built for the name of the LORD."*

David could have been content to teach Solomon and then take full credit for Solomon's success; after all, he taught him everything he knew!

But that wasn't David's heart. His heart was to make his ceiling Solomon's floor, to have Solomon outdo him and surpass him. So he gathered strong, capable men around Solomon and told them, "You work for him now, do everything you can to make him shine!"

The friend I mentioned earlier did the same for me. When we started planning our conferences, he not only allowed me to take charge of them and plan them, including helping me pick speakers, but he also went to the speakers and told them to work with me and make sure the conferences succeed. Following David's example, he worked to ensure I received help from a multitude of sources, not just him. He sets an example we can all follow.

4. DAVID PRAYED FOR SOLOMON TO SUCCEED

Read 1 Chronicles 29:16–19 (NKJV):

> "O LORD our God, all this abundance that we have prepared to build You a house for Your holy name is from Your hand, and is all Your own. I know also, my God, that You test the heart and have pleasure in uprightness. As for me, in the uprightness of my heart I have willingly offered all these things; and now with joy I have seen Your people, who are present here to offer willingly to You. O LORD God of Abraham, Isaac, and Israel, our fathers, keep this forever in the intent of the thoughts of the heart of Your people, and fix their heart toward You. And give my son Solomon a loyal heart to keep Your commandments and Your testimonies and Your statutes, to do all these things, and to build the temple for which I have made provision."

David made sure to pray for Solomon's success. He understood that no matter how much he prepared for Solomon to succeed, no matter how much he taught Solomon to succeed, and no matter how many people he surrounded Solomon with to help him succeed, that he could never succeed without God's blessing. So David held Solomon up in prayer and asked God to help him accomplish what he was called to do.

Guys, David was an amazing man in his own right and has an amazing legacy. He was Israel's greatest king. His epitaph for all history is "A Man After God's Own Heart." Every king in Israel's history after David was compared to David as to whether he was a success or failure.

But even with this legacy, David had to step aside and let the younger men take over. He had to understand that his job was to let his floor in life be their ceiling, and he had to do all he could to make them soar. If someone as amazing and great as David had to do this, why would we ever think we wouldn't?

A real man of God realizes his true calling in life is not to build kingdoms, it is to train kings!

> A real man of God realizes his true calling in life is not to build kingdoms, it is to train kings! We don't need to rack up accomplishments; we need to rack up successors who can outdo us.

We don't need to rack up accomplishments; we need to rack up successors who can outdo us.

We can never claim true success in life until we have younger men under us surpass us spiritually. We achieve greatest success in God's kingdom when we take off our helmets and become cheerleaders. When we realize this, God's kingdom will be unstoppable. So I encourage you to adapt this motto for life:

"My generation's ceiling is the next generation's floor."

That is the endgame of our decision to get in the game. You see, it isn't about you or me, it is all about them!

- What they do in the kingdom.
- How they grow.
- What they accomplish.

They will be our legacy. They are the reason we need to choose to get off the bench and get into the game!

As we come to a close, I want us to pray one final prayer together.

Dear heavenly Father, my fellow brothers, my teammates, and I come humbly before you today. First we ask you to forgive us of any time we have allowed pride to keep us from pouring ourselves into the next generation.

Father, we have chosen to get into the game; help us to stay in the game and to be worthy mentors to the future generation. Help us to live by the motto "We aren't here to build kingdoms, we're here to train kings!"

Move mightily in us and through us as we all work together to encourage the younger generation to not only get in the game, but to win! In Jesus' name, amen!

TRAINING DRILL

1. Ask God to help you to become a mentor to a younger man.
2. Honestly ask yourself, "What would be my response if a man I am mentoring surpassed me spiritually?" Take this answer to God and ask him to help you to encourage others to go further than you can go.

TWO-A-DAYS

Find an activity at your church, like being a youth worker or a Royal Rangers leader, and start investing in the lives of the younger men in your church, especially the ones who don't have a dad in their lives. Go beyond just working at church and make it a part of your everyday life, being a spiritual father to all boys/teens.

TEAM MEETING

1. How would you have reacted if you were David?

2. What are some ways you can help your younger teammates succeed?

3. What is one lesson you can teach a younger man to help him succeed in God's kingdom?

4. What prayers can you pray for a younger man?

5. What does this phrase mean to you: "A real man of God realizes his true calling in life is not to build kingdoms, it is to train kings!"

6. What stands out to you the most about David's story? What did you learn from studying his game footage?

7. How can we as a group help you?

SMALL GROUP
WORKBOOK

CHAPTER 1

CHOOSING TO GET OFF THE BENCH

We need to step out of the _____ _____ and get in the game!

God can use any man who is _____ to be used! He wants you in the game, making a difference for his kingdom.

What struggle or weakness in your life has kept you in from getting into the game?

If you could do any one thing for God's kingdom, i.e., getting in the game, what would it be?

BULLETIN BOARD MATERIAL

It doesn't matter who you are, where you came from, what you have done, or what you are struggling with—there is hope for you! God can use any man who is willing to be used!

TEAM MEETING

1. What does it mean to you to "get in the game?

2. What is the difference between going to church and getting in the game?

3. What is the the biggest obstacle to overcome in your life to get in the game?

4. Will we as a group commit to not only getting in the game but working together to win?

5. How can we as a group help you to get in the game?

CONTRACT BETWEEN YOU AND GOD

(AND YOUR MEN'S GROUP IF WORKING TOGETHER AS A GROUP):

Will you commit to:

Reading each chapter, including Scripture verses? Yes/No

Praying the prayers at the end of the chapter? Yes/No

Completing the Homework Assignments? Yes/No

Sincerely examining your heart against the questions at the end of each chapter? Yes/No

I, _____, am committed to getting out of the comfort of the locker room and getting in the game. I affirm this decision with my signature.

_____

(Sign)   (Date)

CHAPTER 2

LEARNING THE FUNDAMENTALS

There is power when God's men pray. Our prayers could

_____ the _____ if we only took time to pray

them.

The Bible is the _____ _____ we watch to learn

how to defeat the enemy.

Why is it so important for a man of God to spend time in the Word?

What are three practical steps you can take to ensure you daily spend

time in the Word?

    1.

    2.

    3.

BULLETIN BOARD MATERIAL

We need to learn the fundamentals of being a man of God. The two

basic fundamentals we need to excel at are prayer and Bible Reading.

TRAINING DRILL

1. Download the Bible App to your smart phone or device.

2. Find a daily Bible reading plan from someplace like the Bible App or biblegateway.com and commit to reading the Bible daily.

TWO-A-DAYS

Read through the entire Psalm 119 and make a list of all the ways that the psalmist says God's Word makes a difference in our lives.

TEAM MEETING

1. Why are the fundamentals so important?

2. How is your prayer life?

3. How can we as a group help you grow your prayer life?

4. Which of the eight points listed on how to read the Bible do you already use?

5. Which of the eight points are you going to start using?

6. How can we as a group help you develop the fundamentals?

CHAPTER 3

DRAFT DAY

The rich young ruler rejected Jesus because he wanted to serve God the way he _____ to do it. He wanted to stay

_____.

While it hurts to cut out the things that cause a _____ heart, it in no way equals the pain and disappointment that we endure when we realize that we could have had more with _____.

Is there something in your life that you are holding on to that is keeping you from all that God has for you? If so, what is it?

What is the worst thing that could happen if you let it go?

What steps can you take in your life to follow God wholeheartedly, holding nothing back?
1.
2.
3.

BULLETIN BOARD MATERIAL

In order to get into the game, we have to be willing to follow God wholeheartedly, holding nothing back!

200

TRAINING DRILL

Ask God to reveal to you areas that you are not wholeheartedly following him.

Make a list of any areas that are not completely surrendered to God. Then repent of them and make any necessary changes.

TWO-A-DAYS

Ask your mentor and/or a trusted friend or family member if he sees an area in your life where you are not wholeheartedly devoted to God or have a tendency to go back to your old life. Don't be defensive when he honestly answers you.

TEAM MEETING

1. What does it mean to follow God wholeheartedly?

2. What are some things that are dividing your heart?

3. We said the young ruler felt Christianity was following a list of rules and regulations. What is it really?

4. What is keeping you from the blessing of becoming God's man? Is there sin which you are holding on to? Is there something that you are holding on to, something that you won't surrender to God?

5. What are you willing to give up for God? What are you willing to separate yourself from for him?

6. How far will you go for God? Really, how far?

7. What stands out to you the most about the rich young ruler's story? What did you learn from studying his game footage to help you avoid the trap he fell into in his life?

8. How can we as a group help you?

CHAPTER 4

LEAVING THE OLD BEHIND

We have to let go of our _____ if we are going to excel in our _____.

Basically, your "Lot" is the thing that keeps you from 100 percent wholehearted _____ and _____ to God and where he is leading you.

Do you have a relationship that causes you to stay stuck in your old way of life? If so, what steps can you take to make sure this relationship doesn't continue to keep you from following God wholeheartedly?

Is your "Lot" a bondage or sin that you struggle to overcome? Right down what the bondage is and four steps you can take to overcome it:
  1.
  2.
  3.
  4

BULLETIN BOARD MATERIAL

The only way to excel in your walk with God is leaving your old life behind. To fully get in the game, you need to leave your "Lot" behind you once and for all!

TRAINING DRILL

We discussed the need to leave old relationships and friendships behind that are influencing us in a negative way. Ask a trusted mentor or family mentor if he sees any such relationships in your life. Then, as painful as it may be, walk away from these relationships. Pray for these friends, but limit your interaction with them.

TWO-A-DAYS

Join a small group at your church. You need to develop relationships with like-minded believers who can help you in your walk with God. No man is an island, and we need to surround ourselves with fellow believers.

TEAM MEETING

1. What is your "Lot," or the thing from your past that you struggle to leave behind you?

2. How can you leave your negative relationships behind while still reflecting the love of Jesus to these people?

3. Who do you enjoy spending time with, fellow believers or un-believers?

4. What sins or bondages from your past do you struggle to over-come?

5. What stands out to you the most about Abraham's story? What did you learn from studying his game footage to help you avoid the trap he fell into in his life?

6. How can we as a group help you?

CHAPTER 5

PLAYING BY THE RULES

We need to make sure that we do more than just _____
like a follower of God—we have to actually _____ him.

God doesn't have special people who get special _____.
Believing that rules don't apply to you is simply a way of rationalizing away sin. Like Samson, living with this attitude will ultimately
destroy you.

Samson felt that God has special rules for special people. Do you have
any areas in your life that you have been excusing instead of overcoming? If so, what changes do you need to make?

Who are your most trusted friends? Do they steer you to God's ways
or the worlds ways? Write down each friend, and then write down his
true influence.

1.
2.
3.

BULLETIN BOARD MATERIAL

God doesn't have special rules for special people. We all have to do
things his way to be on his team. It isn't enough to just look like we

are part of the team. Our inside lives need to match our outward appearance.

TRAINING DRILL

1. At the end of this chapter we listed some reflective questions. Honestly answer each question. Take time with the Holy Spirit and allow him to show you areas of your life that need to change based on your answers.

2. Ask a trusted friend or mentor how they would answer those questions for you. Don't be defense with their reply, instead honestly accept their feedback and take their advice on ways to change.

TWO-A-DAYS

One of Samson's biggest weakness was he consistently spent his time with bad influences instead of with his fellow Israelites. Commit to developing relationships with other believers. Join a small group at your church and begin doing life with other believers.

TEAM MEETING

1. Have you ever struggled with feeling like God's rules are a hassle?

2. What do you do when you feel this way?

3. Who is your support system in life, believers or unbelievers?

4. Who do you prefer to spend your time with?

5. What stands out to you the most about Samson's story? What did you learn from studying his game footage to help you avoid the trap he fell into in his life?

6. How can we as a group help you?

CHAPTER 6

NO PAIN, NO GAIN

"Be careful not to compromise what you want _____ for what you want _____." —Zig Ziglar

Unlike Esau, Daniel refused to trade God's blessing for

_____ - _____ satisfaction.

We discussed Esau's pursuit of instant gratification. In what area do you struggle to get what you want when you want it?

It is important to think all the way through things: what could be consequences of you doing whatever it takes to get this desire met in your life?

What are three steps you can take to make sure that instant gratification doesn't destroy you?

1.
2.
3.

BULLETIN BOARD MATERIAL

In order to excel in God's kingdom, we have to deny our selfish desires, or weaknesses, and our need to have what we want when we want it, and commit to a life of hard work and perseverance. Instant gratification can have no place in the life of a godly man!

TRAINING DRILL

We ended this chapter asking the question, "In light of eternity, how have we given ground to instant gratification?" Spend time with the Holy Spirit and allow him to show you areas in your life were you are entertaining instant gratification. Write them down. Then think through what the end result could be. Make changes to avoid these consequences.

TWO-A-DAYS

We discussed how debt is a form of instant gratification. Commit yourself to start getting out of debt. Read Dave Ramsey's *Total Money Makeover* and begin the process of getting control of your finances so your finances don't control you.

TEAM MEETING

1. In your own words, define *instant gratification*.

2. Instant gratification can take many shapes and forms. What areas do you struggle most with when it comes to instant gratification?

3. How is debt a form of instant gratification?

4. How did Daniel's choices differ from Esau's? What can we learn from these differences?

5. At the end of the chapter we asked, "Are we trading God's long-term blessing for short-term satisfaction?" What is your answer to this question?

6. What stands out to you the most about Esau's story? What did you learn from studying his game footage to help you avoid the trap he fell into in his life?

7. How can we as a group help you overcome?

CHAPTER 7

WINNERS NEVER CHEAT, AND CHEATERS NEVER WIN

When we practice lying and deceit we are worshiping

_____, the father of _____.

_____ _____ is built on perfect

truth. He can have no part in _____.

How has deceit been a part of your life? Be specific.

Why is deceit so dangerous? How does it affect your witness?

What are three steps you can take to overcome deceit in your life?
   1.
   2.
   3.

BULLETIN BOARD MATERIAL

Nothing shines the light of God into a dark world than being an honest, truthful man. The world doesn't bat an eye when someone lies, they are use to it, but they notice a man of honor and integrity. Be that man!

TRAINING DRILL

1. Start being hard on yourself. Whenever you say something that is not 100 percent true, immediately correct yourself and speak the truth.

2. Grab a concordance or do an online search to see what the Bible says about deceit and lying. As you read each verse, allow the Holy Spirit to convict you of lies you have told in the past. Spend time repenting of these lies, and ask God to change your heart so you only speak words of truth.

TWO-A-DAYS

In this chapter, we discussed times God made me go and apologize to others I had lied to in the past. Allow the Holy Spirit to show you people you have lied to, and humbly go and confess the sin to them and ask them to forgive you.

TEAM MEETING

1. How does deceit affect our relationship with God?

2. How does it affect our relationships with those around us?

3. How does it affect our witness to the lost?

4. How does God feel about deceit?

5. What stands out to you the most about Jacob's story? What did you learn from studying his game footage to help you avoid the trap he fell into in his life?

6. How can we as a group help you?

CHAPTER 8

WINNING AGAINST COMPROMISE

Compromise means to know something is _____
and _____ to do it _____.

Too many believers are getting as close to the line as they can.
However, this is dangerous. Each time we compromise, the line
_____ a little bit. Eventually, we are so far over the line that
we can't _____ _____ it anymore.

What are some decisions or actions we have taken that we knew were
wrong, but we did it anyway?

When did you make this decision? What were you doing? What was
going on in your life at the time?

What steps can you take to break free from your compromise?

BULLETIN BOARD MATERIAL

The good news about compromise is that at any time we can stop
doing it. We must destroy all compromise in our life before it destroys
us.

TRAINING DRILL

At the end of this chapter we listed some questions to ask yourself. Take time to get alone with the Holy Spirit and a notepad. Allow him to show you the truthful answer to the questions. Write down areas you have compromised, repent of them and commit to change.

TWO-A-DAYS

Share the list you made in the homework section with a trusted friend or mentor and ask him to hold you accountable. Also, ask him if he sees areas of compromise in you that you missed.

TEAM MEETING

1. Define *compromise.*

2. In this chapter we said, "Each time we compromise just a little, it makes it easier to do it again." What does this mean to you?

3. Are there areas of compromise that have crept into your life?

4. How has compromised affected the church community?

5. What can we as a group do to keep compromise from destroying our men's group and our church community?

6. How do we defeat compromise?

7. What stands out to you the most about Solomon's story? What did you learn from studying his game footage to help you avoid the trap he fell into in his life?

8. How can we as a group help you?

CHAPTER 9

SHINING A LIGHT ON THE DARK CORNERS

Until we consecrate ourselves and _____

_____ _____, we won't experience the blessing of God in our lives or defeat our spiritual enemies.

The best way to overcome hidden sins is to become

_____.

Do you have any secret sin in your life? What is it?

Think all the way through your secret sin: what could be the consequences of someone else exposing your hidden sins?

In order to break free of secret sin, you need to confess it. Who can you tell your secret sin to so it loses its hold on your life? Who has this sin affected that you need to tell?

BULLETIN BOARD MATERIAL

It is time for men of God to stand up and say enough is enough! It is time for men of God to shine the light of truth on their lives and to gain freedom from their secret sins. It is time we stand up and say "I am trapped in sin, I want to be free, and I don't care who knows it!"

TRAINING DRILL

The only way to remove hidden sin is to expose it. After you confess your sin to God, find a *mature, trustworthy* believer and confess your sin to him. Ask him to help you overcome.

TWO-A-DAYS

Secret sin is so dangerous because only you and God know about it. Blow this to smithereens by opening yourself to accountability. Meet weekly with an accountability partner and allow him to ask you anything he wants about any area of your life and answer him honestly.

TEAM MEETING

1. What is the danger of hidden sins?

2. Why does Satan want to expose secret sins?

3. Why does God want to expose secret sins?

4. How can secret sins affect our families?

5. How can secret sins affect our small group?

6. How can secret sins affect our church?

7. What place does accountability have in defeating secret sins?

8. Knowing that what happens in the group stays in the group, does anyone have anything they need to confess after reading this chapter?

CHAPTER 10

TRUTH IN BLACK & WHITE, AND ALL COLORS IN BETWEEN

Prejudice is really concealed _____.

All people have this same basic _____

_____ no matter their age, race, sex, or social position.

We all wrestle with some form of prejudice. What would be your area of prejudice?

How could your prejudice cause someone to not come to Jesus?

What are three practical steps we can take to overcome our prejudice?
1.
2.
3.

BULLETIN BOARD MATERIAL

A true man of God has nothing but love and respect in his heart for all people, no matter there age, race, sex, or social position. There is no room for ANY prejudice inside of God's man!

TRAINING DRILL

We discussed in this chapter how some churches are prejudiced against young people. Think about your church. Can you see ways that young people may feel unwelcome or unwanted in your church? Write them down, then ask God to give you a plan to fight against this so that they feel welcome, wanted, and loved.

TWO-A-DAYS

If your church has a group for young adults (i.e., older than the youth group, nineteen– to thirty-year-olds), volunteer to serve in this group. if your church doesn't have anything for this age group, start something and commit to loving and accepting this age group into your church.

TEAM MEETING

1. We all wrestle with some form of prejudice. What would be your area of prejudice?

2. We made the statement in this chapter that, "when we allow prejudice to have a place in our lives, we are giving ground to hatred." What do you think of this statement?

3. How does prejudice relate to the fact that young people are leaving the church?

4. What can you do about this?

5. What can we as a group do about it?

6. What stands out to you the most about Jonah's story? What did you learn from studying his game footage to help you avoid the trap he fell into in his life?

7. How can we as a group help you?

CHAPTER 11

PLAYING THROUGH DISAPPOINTMENT

Judas couldn't get past his disappointment that Jesus didn't do things
_____ _____.

Overcoming disappointment is a _____ battle.

What are some differences between how Judas and Job handled disappointment?

How has disappointment affected your spiritual life?

How does gratitude combat disappointment?

What are some things you can be grateful for?

BULLETIN BOARD MATERIAL

We must choose to be sons who submit to God and follow him wholeheartedly no matter where he leads. We need to trust that he knows more than us and will work things out for our good. This is the only way to receive God's blessing in our lives.

TRAINING DRILL

We all face some form of disappointment in our lives. Looking back at your life, how did you react in your time of disappointment? Be honest with yourself and with God. Make a list of any sins or compromises you committed and ask God to forgive you.

TWO-A-DAYS

The best way to overcome disappointment is through exercising one thing—gratitude. Make a comprehensive list of things you can be grateful for. When disappointment rears its ugly head, use your grateful list to combat it. You will be surprised how dwelling on things to be grateful for defeats feelings of disappointment.

TEAM MEETING

1. Have you ever been disappointed in how God did something in your life?

2. Have feelings that you deserved better caused you to feel like you deserve to commit sins or do things you know you shouldn't do?

3. Have you acted on your feelings?

4. Did you overcome your disappointment? If so, how?

5. What stands out to you the most about the rich Judas' story? What did you learn from studying his game footage to help you avoid the trap he fell into in his life?

6. How can we as a group help you?

CHAPTER 12

THE VALUE OF A GOOD COACH

God never intended man to go through life _____. His will is for the _____ men to take the wisdom and experience they gained and use it to help the _____ men _____ them spiritually.

God wants his men to learn and glean everything we can from each other. He wants us to strive to _____ our mentor because we avoid the _____ they experienced. We are to learn everything we possibly can so we can become all God created us to be.

Who is your mentor? What are some of the lessons you have learned from him?

Is there any area you are holding back being open with your mentor? If so, why? what is holding you back?

BULLETIN BOARD MATERIAL

One of God's greatest gifts is the gift of a mentor. It is our job to take full advantage of this gift and submit ourselves to them. We need to learn from them so we can become all God created us to be!

TRAINING DRILL

If you are not currently in a mentoring relationship, immediately seek out a mentor in your life.

If you have a mentor, ask him to forgive you for anytime you didn't embrace his wisdom and advice.

TWO-A-DAYS

Ask your mentor the questions we listed at the end of the chapter and accept his responses to you. Reaffirm to him your commitment to the mentoring relationship and your willingness to change.

TEAM MEETING

1. Do you have a mentor? How did you meet?

2. Why is it a good thing to have a mentor?

3. This chapter listed some ways men struggle to take full advantage of a mentor relationship. What is your biggest struggle?

4. How can you overcome this struggle?

5. What is your biggest fear about being mentored?

6. Is this a rational fear? What can you do to overcome?

7. What stands out to you the most about Gehazi's story? What did you learn from studying his game footage to help you avoid the trap he fell into in his life?

8. How can we as a group work together to encourage mentorship?

9. Is there a man you can be a mentor to?

CHAPTER 13

BEING A TEAM PLAYER

Our teammates supply _____ to us. They provide a way
for us to have _____ in our lives.

God's will is men helping _____, showing other men
what you learned on your journey to _____.

Who are your teammates, your band of brothers?

What are three ways you and your teammates can commit to helping
each other grow in your walk with God?
   1.
   2.
   3.

Who can you add to your team? How will you do it?

BULLETIN BOARD MATERIAL

None of us were meant to live this life alone. Just like even the greatest football player in the world can't win the game without his teammates, we can't become all God wants us to be unless we are part of a team. It's the way God designed it!

TRAINING DRILL

Make a list of your teammates. Think of three ways these each man has helped you grow spiritually in your walk with God. Then send each of them a note thanking them.

TWO-A-DAYS

Find a guy at your church who hasn't really connected yet and make him one of your teammates. That way you and the rest of the guys on your team can help him feel like he belongs and has a place in the church family.

TEAM MEETING

1. "No man is an island." What does this statement mean to you?

2. Does the thought of having men in your life who can ask you anything or hold you accountable freak you out? Why?

3. Who is someone who has invested in your life?

4. How has his investment benefited you?

5. Who is a new man at your church you and your group can reach out to and include onto your team?

CHAPTER 14

BUILDING THE TEAM FOR THE FUTURE

Our generation's _____ is the next generation's

_____.

We need to give the younger men an example to try and

_____, and then we need to celebrate with them

when they _____ us.

Who are you mentoring? Who could you be mentoring?

What can you do to help a younger man succeed in God's kingdom?

List five ways you can pray for the younger man you're mentoring.
   1.
   2.
   3.
   4.
   5.

BULLETIN BOARD MATERIAL

A real man of God realizes his true calling in life is not to build king-doms, it is to train kings! We don't need to rack up accomplishments; we need to rack up successors who can outdo us.

TRAINING DRILL

1. Ask God to help you to become a mentor to an younger man.

2. Honestly ask yourself, "What would be my response if a man I am mentoring surpassed me spiritually? Take this answer to God and ask God to help you to encourage others to go further than you can go.

TWO-A-DAYS

Find an activity at your church, like being a youth worker or a Royal Rangers leader, and start investing in the lives of the younger men in your church, especially the ones who don't have a dad in their lives. Go beyond just working at church and make it a part of your every-day life, being a spiritual father to all boys/teens.

TEAM MEETING

1. How would you have reacted if you were David?

2. What are some ways you can help your younger teammates succeed?

3. What is one lesson you can teach a younger man to help him succeed in God's kingdom?

4. What prayers can you pray for a younger man?

5. What does this phrase mean to you: "A real man of God realizes his true calling in life is not to build kingdoms, it is to train kings!"

6. What stands out to you the most about David's story? What did you learn from studying his game footage?

7. How can we as a group help you?

WORKBOOK FILL-IN ANSWERS

CHAPTER 1

    1. locker room 2. willing

CHAPTER 2

    1. change, world 2. game tape

CHAPTER 3.

    1. wanted, comfortable 2. divided, God

CHAPTER 4

    1. past, future 2. surrender, abandonment

CHAPTER 5

    1. look, follow 2. rules

CHAPTER 6

    1. most, now 2. short term

CHAPTER 7

    1. Satan, lies 2. God's kingdom, deceit

CHAPTER 8

    1. wrong, choosing, anyway 2. moves, even see

CHAPTER 9

    1. remove the sin 2. tattletales

GET IN THE GAME

CHAPTER 10

    1. hate 2. spiritual need

CHAPTER 11

    1. his way 2. mental

CHAPTER 12

    1. alone, older, younger, surpass 2. outdo, pitfalls

CHAPTER 13

    1. support, accountability 2. men, manhood

CHAPTER 14

    1. ceiling, floor 2. surpass, surpass

Jamie loves to speak to men and is available to speak at your next men's event. Jamie combines humor and his personal testimony to both engage and challenge men to grow in their walk with God. He uses his testimony of overcoming abuse as well as dealing with his physical and emotional issues growing up to encourage men that no matter what their background or where they have come from in life, they can grow into mighty men in God's kingdom.

"Years ago, while I was attending the University of Valley Forge, God gave me a deep desire to minister to men. My calling is to help men learn what it means to be a godly man and how to develop a deep, personal relationship with their heavenly Father. We strive to challenge and encourage men to reach their full potential in God's kingdom."

If you are interested in having Jamie at your next men's event as a speaker or workshop leader, or if you are interested in having him come share with your church, e-mail him at jamie@mantourministries.com. He is also available to speak for one or multiple weeks on the theme of his books, *Putting On Manhood, Legacy: Living a Life that Lasts,* and *Get in the Game.*

If you enjoyed this book, why not buy a copy for
a man in prison.
You can help us reach more men behind bars
by donating at
MANTOURMINISTRIES.COM.

Mantour Ministries donates copies of our
curriculum to state and federal prisons.

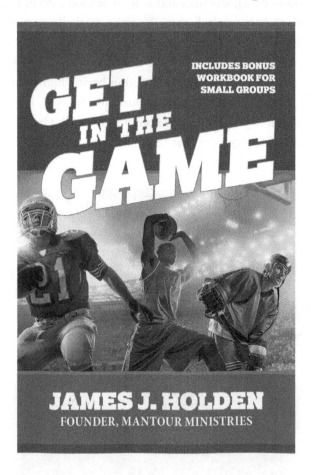

We are reaching men behind bars
with the gospel!

ALSO FOR MEN

Will you leave behind a good legacy or a bad legacy? By reading the stories of men from the Bible, working through the study questions and the legacy challenges in each chapter, you'll be well on your way to living a life that lasts. Excellent for individual or small group study.

Visit **mantourministries.com** for details.

Also available in both print and digital formats
from Amazon, BarnesandNoble.com,
and other online retailers.

ALSO BY JAMES HOLDEN

This book will show you how to put childish ways behind you and become the man God designed you to be. Each chapter provides questions for reflection, making it an excellent tool for individual or small group study.

Visit **mantourministries.com** for details.

Also available in both print and digital formats
from Amazon, BarnesandNoble.com,
and other online retailers.